Crossing the Catwalk: Transvestism in Contemporary Fashion and Culture

Laura Cherrie Beaney

Crossing the Catwalk: Transvestism in Contemporary Fashion and Culture

Laura Cherrie Beaney

Academica Press
Washington - London

Library of Congress Cataloging-in-Publication Data

Names: Beaney, Laura Cherrie, author.
Title: Crossing the catwalk : transvestism in contemporary fashion and
    culture / Laura Cherrie Beaney.
Description: London ; Washington, DC : Academica Press, 2019. |
Includes
    bibliographical references.
Identifiers: LCCN 2018055596| ISBN 9781680534801 (hardcover : alk.
paper)
    | ISBN 9781680534825 (pbk. : alk. paper)
Subjects: LCSH: Cross-dressing.
Classification: LCC HQ77 .B43 2019 | DDC 306.77/8--dc23
LC record available at https://lccn.loc.gov/2018055596

For my father, best friend, kindest critic, and constant motivator Peter W. Beaney.

His wisdom prevails: "Be good and if you can't be good be fabulous."

Contents

Introduction

In the 1930s, Sigmund Freud observed, "When you meet a human being, the first distinction you make is 'male or female?' and you are accustomed to make the distinction with unhesitating certainty." (Bolich, 2007: 55)

As Freud suggests, society is divisible by gender. We are taken to be either "male" or "female." This notion seems to be fixed within our culture and is often unquestioned. In medical science, for example, it is taken for granted that there are anatomical and psychological differences that separate men from women. Before we are born we are identified as a "boy" or a "girl;" after birth boys are stereotypically dressed in blue and girls are dressed in pink, and each gender is expected to act and behave in a certain way, based upon their gender. Indeed, the idea of a binary gender is embedded within Western culture. It is present in Christianity,[1] in schooling and the workplace,[2] in art, in literature, and in the eyes of the law. Commercially, too, there is a distinct gender divide, as we see specific products, garments, and advertisements aimed at either men or women.

---

[1] Christianity is a religion that prescribes different roles in the church according to gender, with the most important roles traditionally afforded to men.

[2] In many countries females often earn less than their male counterparts.

As fixed as it may seem, gender as a concept and practice is also challenged and contested. If we look at the idea of color, for example, it is apparent that although, as noted above, the use of color is deeply gendered, ideas about color are not as fixed as they initially seem, and perceptions have changed cross-culturally and over the course of time. Deep-rooted ideas about gender are often put into place during childhood. In contemporary Western culture, we are taught from an early age that it is natural for girls to wear pink and for boys to wear blue. Prior to the 1940s, however, boys were dressed in pink, a color deemed to be "stronger," and girls wore blue, a color worn by the Virgin Mary, which was thought to be "delicate" and "pure" – the opposite, in fact, of what we see today. Even more surprisingly, up until the 1920s children's attire was not color-coded at all and all children were dressed in a similar type of gown, regardless of gender. According to Jo Paoletti of the University of Maryland, "in the era before domestic washing machines all babies wore white as a practical matter, since the only way of getting clothes clean was to boil them." (Paoletti: 2011)

Colors have carried a varied range of meanings. Garber recalls that in the 1950s the color green was considered to be the "homosexual" color, while today, she argues, it is lavender or pink. The color pink was used by Nazis in the Second World War to mark out homosexual men, but is now "defiantly 'inverted' by gay activists on t-shirts and buttons as a sign of gay pride ... Pink now identifies - when they choose it to - gay men and lesbians. What goes around comes around." (Garber: 1992:2) More generally, gender identities have also been fluid, and again, differ according to location, time, and culture. During the English Renaissance, for example, it was commonplace for men to wear frilled and jewelled clothing, whereas during the Victorian period such detailing was seen to be an extremely feminine trait; men wore a simplified, austere style of dress. Before the Second World War, men stereotypically wore trousers, while women, whose lives did not demand the type of movement that came with trousers, were expected to wear skirts or dresses. This illustrates the way in which our perceptions of gender change to reflect the society we live in.

While gender is relatively fixed within our society, we are nevertheless entertained by "gender bending." The media and entertainment industries contest and represent a range of gender identities. The popularity of television dames such as Danny La Rue (1927-2009) and Dame Edna Everage, who performed at the Queen of England's Jubilee celebration in 2002, and filmic representations such as *Some Like It Hot* (1959), *Tootsie* (1982) and *Big Momma's House* (2000) reinforce the idea that society has been fascinated by the idea of blending genders for a long time.

As much as it is a cultural phenomenon, gender is also an individual practice. Social theorists describe some apparently "deviant" individuals as "gender outlaws," as they exist on the margins of society and challenge the stereotypes that come with gender. These individuals actively choose to blend and shape their own gender identities. This might consist of "dressing-up" in privacy or seeking group affiliation in clubs and social movements. The reasons that the individual might wish to experiment with their gender are varied. It could be for creative or entertainment purposes; for social, political, religious or personal reasons; or even, in the case of the lady-boys of Thailand, for example, for prostitution. It is clear then that while the medical world seeks to assign the individual to a specific gender, there are some who do not believe they fit into either category and describe themselves as "pan gender" or a third gender. For these people, the possibility of "bending" the idea of gender or of "blending" the assigned characteristics of the two genders can be very attractive. As Plummer (1996) suggests, although gender categories have been challenged in the past by transvestites and transgendered persons, there is now "a much more culturally challenging form" of gender questioning at work. In the activities of "the 'blenders' who transcend, transgress and threaten" stereotypes, there seems to be a desire to find "a world of multiple gendered fluidities – a world at home in a postmodern, cacophony of multiplicity, pastiche and pluralities." (Plummer: 1996: xvi)

If we refer back to Freud's observation, we see that although most people regard gender as fixed, many in fact question and contest gender identities for social, cultural, medical, and political reasons. Fashion, the main focus of this dissertation, is one of the areas of popular culture in which people contest the idea of gender. This can be seen in a multitude of ways, ranging from the creation of images and the design of clothing lines to the construction of individual style.

Fashionable clothing makes multiple statements about the wearer. It can identify social status and tell the viewer, "This is the type of person I am." One of the strongest messages that clothing can convey, however, is the gender identity of the wearer. Crane describes how the upper-class woman of the nineteenth century would dress to fit her gendered role: "The ideal role of the upper-class woman, who was not expected to work inside or outside the home, was reflected in the ornamental and impractical nature of the clothing styles." (Crane: 2000, 16) According to Simmel's analysis of the fashion system in his work on "leisured society," middle

and working-class women would attempt to emulate the styles of the upper class because fashions were established at the peak of the class system and handed down hierarchically. This did, however, cause problems, particularly for the lower-class woman, who was expected to perform manual work, as the clothing styles deemed appropriate and fashionable for women – which were designed for leisured use - were restrictive and imposed constraints upon her social and gendered role in life. (Crane: 2000)

In contemporary culture fashion designers, stylists, photographers and the media have been fascinated with the idea of gender and the ever-changing boundaries between what constitutes "masculine" or "feminine." Fashion is, as Arnold notes, the most "instant means of asserting or subverting the once stable masculine/feminine divide." (Arnold: 2001) The fashion industry is, in part, responsible for reinforcing and challenging gender stereotypes: "When, for example, we mock our male friends for wearing a shirt that is a bit 'girly,' complex theories of gender, social status, and communication lie behind what we say, usually without our knowing it." (Barnard: 2007:1)

Both men and women have crossed the barriers between the genders in terms of adopting elements of each other's styles as much in the past as in the present. According to a fairly recent edition of *Elle* magazine, for example, "Coco Chanel loved a girl in boy's clothes - and her brand of chic subversion is everywhere this season. Think masculine suiting, tweed, a classic white shirt, brogues, a trilby hat." (*Elle*, Autumn/Winter 2011, *The Runway Edit*, p. 5) This is not so much transvestism, in the sense men and women cross-dressing to become the other sex, but rather, as postmodernists would have it, women appropriating male style and dress. Examples of this proliferate. If we look at recent history, for example, we can see how in 1966 Yves Saint Laurent's iconic *le Smoking* tuxedo was said to "liberate" fashionable women, allowing them to dress in clothes that were previously the domain of upper-class men and feminists. In 1986, Katharine Hamnett's Power Dressing collection also influenced thousands of women to emulate men's style and assert masculine power in the workplace. As Arnold suggests, once the "traditional molds" have been broken, they cannot be replaced (Arnold: 2001). Images of masculinity have also been susceptible to change within fashion. Pip McCormac's account of buying his first pair of "sensible" shoes illustrates, for example, the way in which the ideals of what fashion considers to be masculine can change very rapidly: "I bought my first pair of proper, grown-up shoes. From Bottega Veneta and in brown leather, with a pointy end and an ever-so-slight lift in the heel, they were not what my father would have classified as 'men's shoes' 10 years ago." (McCormac: 2009)

While it was common in the past for men and women to "borrow" elements associated with the opposite gender for the purposes of work, fantasy, or recreation, in the present day, the media encourages us to think that it is more acceptable to "play" with perceptions of gender. As Hollander (1994) observed in the 1990s, "Both sexes play changing games today, because for the first time in centuries men are learning clothing habits from women, instead of the other way around." In consumer culture, we can see how it has become more acceptable for men and women to express alternative identities. Makeup for men has appeared at various intervals throughout history; glam rockers and new romantics wore makeup in the 1970s and 1980s; and today male models on the catwalks and celebrities such as Russell Brand and Noel Fielding are often seen wearing makeup. However, for the first time we are seeing makeup specifically designed for men, selling at high and low levels of fashion: Jean-Paul Gaultier and Clinique both offer premium rate "makeup for men," while high street stores such as Superdrug sell the Taxi Man makeup line for men, which offers men's mascara among other products at affordable prices. The idea of body adornment is also no longer solely associated with femininity; stores such as Topman and River Island stock items of jewelry for men that include necklaces, bracelets, and earrings, and rock star Pete Doherty recently collaborated with Joseph to create a range of upscale men's jewelry.

In recent years the fashion industry has also been focused upon ideas of unisex and androgyny. This goes beyond transvestism because, as Arnold (2001: 122) notes, "while unisex seeks to mask the body in supposedly genderless clothes, androgyny seeks to unite male and female, masculine and feminine in one body." In this vein, in 1994 Calvin Klein launched a cleverly marketed campaign, photographed by Steven Meisel, to front the CK One scent, which was aimed at both men and women. In 2011 Meisel was again enlisted to photograph Calvin Klein's first CK One collection to include clothing, underwear, and fragrance. The shoot features a range of contemporary faces, from Pixie Geldof to boxing champion Robert Evans, who are sent to try on the collection in a mirrored room in a way that exemplifies the comments on "playing changing games" made above:

> We put the pieces in there in all sizes, from XXXL to XS; it's not about the perfect size - it's a play on proportion and androgyny. Girls were wearing jeans that were baggy and

far too big, or wearing oversized shirts as dresses, they made the collection their own. It's the personalisation of fashion - and the campaign is really just a reportage of them trying the clothes." (Carrigan: 2011)

During the twentieth century, the emergence of mass production and consumption served to hide or mask some of the ways in which we distinguish between different members of society. Categories such as class and social status are, arguably, no longer as powerful as they were in the past, though different styles of consumption and abilities to consume may have replaced or hidden these distinctions. Gender barriers, however, still serve, at least within the dominant sectors of society, to distinguish between the two sexes and are still influential in terms of how individuals are treated and categorised, despite – or possibly in response to – the blending of categories noted above. This creates conflict, contradiction, and anxiety amid characteristics that some see as exemplifying an ongoing transition from a modern to a "postmodern" society. Arnold describes this process in terms of how, in the 1990s, in high and low fashion, there was a denial of "difference:" "The diversity of contemporary culture and the break-up of existing ideas of gender, race, and sexuality [has] led to confusion surrounding definitions of identity [and] uncertainty surrounding gender identities has frequently been accompanied by a more functional way of dressing." (Arnold: 2001:118)

This "functionality" can arguably be seen in trends such as androgyny and unisex, which are associated with periods of cultural anxiety over gender and the challenging of gender divides. The use of "new" gender identities has, however, been a particularly marked aspect of contemporary fashion and popular culture generally – as the above examples illustrate. Indeed, the fashion industry seems to afford a sense of power as well as decadence to alternative gender identities. This is what Whitworth describes as a "movement in fashion to blur gender boundaries" (Whitworth: 2010). If we look to the covers of contemporary fashion publications, the imagery is very different to what we have seen in the last decade. Now we see a range of different gender identities and means of expression outside the traditional binary gender divide. The January 2011 "androgyny" issue of *Love* magazine featured transgender supermodel Lea T and Kate Moss kissing. In a similar manner, in the September issue of *Vogue Hommes* (Japan), Nick Knight photographed global icon Lady Gaga in drag as her male alter-ego, Jo Calderone. The slogan on the front cover read "Too cool to care." Knight shot two alternative covers for Vogue, one showing Jo Calderone in smart attire and the other in casual dress. Rather than creating a "look" for aesthetic reasons, Lady Gaga has taken this idea a step further and constructed a new male persona for herself. In her *Vogue* interview she speaks as Calderone and details his background and ambitions:

> "Where are you from?"
> "Palermo, Sicily"
> "How would you describe what you do / your occupation?"
> "Mechanic for my dad's business. This is the first time I've had my picture taken."

The singer, who is typically known for reinventing her identity in the public eye, drew upon her alter-ego, Calderone to promote her music release in August 2011. The promotional images for the release and the magazine covers share some similarities in their style and appearance. They have been shot in the traditional "fashion/beauty" black and white mode with the models' faces tilted away from the camera - this makes it difficult to distinguish their true identities. The perspective implies that the purpose of using these alternative genders in fashion is not for shock value, but simply what fashion deems to be "of the moment" and chic, especially when seen on the cover of *Vogue,* the magazine that exemplifies high fashion.

This trend is also apparent within the beauty industry. The majority of makeup and cosmetic brands promote their products by drawing upon the ideals of beauty (sometimes airbrushed) from young, female models. However, MAC[3] makeup has taken a different approach. The brand's motto is: "All Ages, All Races, All Sexes," and rather than using traditional models to promote their products, they opted for non-traditional role models such as drag queen RuPaul, the late Boy George, and what MAC describes as "non-lipstick lesbian" (MAC: 2011) KD Lang.

Fashion designers and stylists have been inspired by alternative gender identities when creating images and when showcasing their designs on the catwalk. Transgender supermodels such as the Brazilian Lea T have been modelling for Italian *Vanity Fair* and photographed nude for French *Vogue*. Male model Andrej Pejic (has been working for Marc Jacobs and Jean-Paul Gaultier in womenswear. In 2010 and again in 2011, Marc Jacobs also appeared on the cover of *Industrie* magazine styled by Katie Grand and photographed by Patrick Demarchelier dressed completely in womenswear. James Franco made a similar statement when he was photographed by Terry Richardson on the cover of *Candy* magazine, the first fashion and style magazine dedicated to transgender, transvestite and

---

[3] A fashionable and high-priced brand of makeup stocked in stores such as Selfridges and Harrods and originally pioneered for black women.

androgynous target audience. As Arnold suggests, "Fashion needs constantly to stay ahead, to entice the consumer with temptations of the new, to distract a culture satiated with imagery by creating visions that experiment with and challenge conventional morality." (Arnold: 2001:125)

In the contemporary period there are many instances in which fashion has challenged, contested, or "played" with the boundaries between what is thought to be "male" or "female." This has been particularly focused around identities and ideas about transvestism, transgenderism, and androgyny. A range of different but related identities has emerged, from those who seek to use transvestism as a way of adopting the opposite gender to those who want to dissolve or abandon the distinctions between genders.

It is, therefore, interesting from a fashion perspective to understand how this mediated image of gender equality in the twenty-first century relates to reality by examining cross-dressing and transvestism through the construction of personal style. In order to gain an understanding of the context in which cross-dressing and transvestism exist, the next section, "History and Context," will examine a wide range of examples of cross-dressing from both males and females in Western history. The following section, "Blending and Bending: Cross-dressing and Androgyny in a 'Postmodern' World," will explore the main ideas and theories surrounding these types of identity in contemporary culture and examine the idea of cross-dressing and drag through the alternative lenses of subcultural and postmodern theory. By using case studies from a range of different sources, the following sections will give a clear idea of how the reality of cross-dressing compares to the glamorous and decadent image portrayed by the fashion industry. It will aim to uncover the true motivations for those who cross-dress and the construction of their personal styles in relation to fashion.

History and Context

Introduction

Although a complete and comprehensive history of cross-dressing falls beyond the scope of this book, this section draws upon key examples to illustrate and examine how society's attitudes towards transvestism and cross-dressing have changed and differ according to culture and period. The examples focus primarily upon Western cultures and practices, with some reference to non-Western societies where appropriate, and help to explore some of the reasons why transvestism may exist, including religion, the pursuit of social freedom, social promotion, and the attempt to appropriate the perceived power of the other gender.

In contemporary society the dominant belief is that the gender is binary and fairly fixed. Cross-dressers and transvestites have, however, continually challenged the boundaries of what society considers to be the gender "norm." We might regard it as a relatively new phenomenon; however, transvestism and cross-dressing have, in fact, been evident in human behavior throughout history.

Cross-dressing in Ancient Cultures: Greece and Rome

Vases dating back to Ancient Greece depict bearded men with earrings and parasols. Miller interprets the vases as "ancient evidence for transvestite activity." (Miller: 1999:223) Other evidence is embedded within Greek mythology. Male priests would, for example, dress as women to honor the "Bearded Aphrodite of Cyprus." (Stryker and Whittle: 2006) Indeed, ancient religions offer numerous examples of transvestism for ritual and religious reasons. Stryker and Whittle describe the way in which men would "dress-up" to participate in the religious events in Ancient Rome:

> Men had to dress up before they could take part in the rites of Hercules at Rome (Hercules spent three years dressed as a woman at the court of Omphale, Queen of Lydia) … At the vine growers' festival, the Athenian Oschophoria, two boys dressed in women's clothes and carried a vine stock in procession. At the Argive festival of Hybristika, the men adopted female clothing. At the feast of Hera at Samos, the men wore long, white robes and placed their hair in golden nets. (Stryker and Whittle: 2006)

Accounts of cross-dressing by women however, have been less common. The most prominent is perhaps the myth of the masculine Amazonian warrior women recounted by Herodotus, which, it has been argued, can be interpreted as a reflection of the deep-rooted anxiety of Greek males about the role of women in their society:

> The basic characteristics of Amazonian society show the Amazons did not fit into the mould of the good Greek woman. Many of the details of Amazonian culture distinctly showed how the women were considered strange and unnatural by the Greeks. (Woods: 2010:14)

Woods describes the Amazon women as, "unsuccessfully playing at the role of men," as it was the men who were expected to be powerful providers for women and go to battle at that time.

Medieval Europe: Aristocrats and "Crossing the Stage" in Shakespeare

In 1431, Joan of Arc demonstrated power and cross-dressed, going against society's divisions, so that she could fight for what she believed in. Dressed as a man, she led an army of 10,000 Frenchmen to battle against the invading English. After Joan was caught, she was forced to admit to "wearing clothing that violated natural decency," among other transgressions. (Stryker and Whittle: 2006) Condemend to death, she was burned at the stake, at least in part, for the crime of transvestitism. Later, however, nobles and aristocrats would openly cross-dress without the threat of death. King Henry III of France (1551-1588) was, for example, famed for cross-dressing as an Amazonian warrior and for encouraging his courtiers to do the same. Bullough and Bullough (1993) note that Henry III would often be seen wearing a "ball-gown, makeup, earrings and other jewelry." The King's mignons, or "favorites," would also wear female clothing. Pierre de L'Estoile, a French chronicler of the time, wrote that the mignons wore their hair "the way whores in a bordello did - pomaded, artificially curled and recurled and flowing back over small velvet bonnets." (Bullough and Bullough: 1993:104).

Cross-dressing was equally represented and even fêted in the arts – not least because this was a protected space for those who lacked the protection afforded by the royal courts and the aristocracy. During the English Renaissance in the sixteenth and seventeenth centuries, cross-dressing on the stage was commonplace. William Shakespeare (1564-1616) created characters of women who cross-dressed as men in his plays *Twelfth Night, The Merchant of Venice,* and *As You Like It.* Sumptuary laws at the time addressed society's fears of men and women dressing, acting, eating, and generally behaving beyond their social positions (Alkin: 2005). The stage, as noted above, was a 'safe' space." Actors on stage were allowed to "violate the sumptuary laws that governed dress and social station." (Garber: 1992:37) Until 1660, only male actors were allowed to perform in public, as it was deemed an inappropriate occupation for women. Male actors, therefore, had to play all female roles. Out of necessity, they transgressed their gender and social status by wearing clothes donated to the theatre by noblemen. They also added gender complexity to the performance as males had to play Shakespeare's crossed-dressed female characters such as Viola in *Twelfth Night* and Rosalind in *As You Like It*. By blurring gender distinctions, what is "real" and "unreal" can become confused and provide dramatic tension as well as challenge assumptions about gender roles.

The Early Modern Period: Eighteenth and Nineteenth Century Western Cross-Dressing

During the eighteenth century Bullough and Bullough (1993) claim that there was an increasing interest in cross-dressing and impersonation in the public domain. Events such as masquerade balls provided a safe environment for men and women to "drop the gender barriers," at least among the elite:

> Men could experiment in safety with gender reversal by dressing as women, primping in furbelows and flounces, while women could express a more masculine character, strutting about in jackboots and breeches. Horace Warpole (1717-97) reported passing as an old woman at a masquerade in 1742, while other males disguised themselves as witches, bawds, nursery-maids, and shepherdesses. (Bullough and Bullough: 1993:126)

There is, however, a difference between those who cross-dress from time-to-time at events such as masquerade balls and those who embrace transvestism as their fulltime identity. The French aristocrat the Chevalier d'Eon[4] (1728-1810) is a prime example of an upper-class cross-dresser of the eighteenth century. Bullough and Bullough describe d'Eon's appearance in a portrait by Angelica Kauffman (the portrait was copied from the work of Maurice Quentin de La Tour, painter to the king) thus: "dressed as a young woman of quality, wearing a dainty lace cap, drop pearl earrings, a black velvet ribbon around his neck, a low, lacy *décolletage* revealing a full breast... It seems clear that the chevalier might well have dressed as a woman early in his career." (Bullough and Bullough: 1993:127)

D'Eon worked for King Louis XV's *Secret*[5] as a spy. On a secret mission to St. Petersburg, he was said to have been formally introduced to society as a young woman. D'Eon was often referred to as "Lia" by his superior, the Marquis de L'Hôpital, which is believed to have been his female name when cross-dressing (Bullough and Bullough: 1993). While in Russia, d'Eon's partner, Chevalier Douglas, is said to have asked him which wardrobe he preferred, to which d'Eon replied, "I would prefer to keep my male clothes, because they open all the doors to fortune, glory, and courage. Dresses close all the doors for me .... nature has come to oppose me, and to make me feel the need for women's clothes." (Kates: 2001:71).

---

[4] Charles-Geneviève-Louis-Auguste-André-Timothée Eon de Beaumont.
[5] Louis XV's *Secret*, also known as *Secret du Roi*, was a secret diplomatic service established in 1745.

In 1763 d'Eon encountered financial difficulties and was forced to borrow money. He made some powerful enemies, and King Louis XV urged him to dress in female clothing as a disguise. At this time rumors spread that d'Eon was actually a woman in disguise. As a means of escaping the punishment for his actions as a man, he announced that he was indeed a woman. King Louis XVI offered d'Eon a pension, which relieved his financial difficulties, but did so on the condition that d'Eon would continue to dress as a woman for the rest of his life. D'Eon wrote plaintively, "I am trying to walk in pointed shoes with high heels but have nearly broken my neck more than once; it has happened that, instead of making a courtesy, I have taken off my wig and three-tiered head-dress, taking them for my hat or my helmet." (Bullough and Bullough: 1993:30)

That d'Eon's gender remained in doubt throughout his life – a tribute perhaps to his disguise – is illustrated by the fact that when d'Eon's housemate, a Mrs. Cole, discovered his body in 1810 she was said to have been in shock when she discovered that he was "unquestionably male." His life, however, has been endlessly discussed and studied by many academics, who are undecided as to whether d'Eon was a transvestite or gender confused. D'Eon's story effectively illustrates, however, how gender roles can easily become ambiguous as well as how this confusion can serve other purposes.

Although female-to-male cross-dressing is relatively hidden compared to the male-to-female version, during the eighteenth and nineteenth centuries there were prominent cases of women adopting male identities for long periods of time. Although this phenomenon has been less studied and less emulated, it seems that female cross-dressing was, in many cases, adopted as much in order to gain employment or access to male dominated institutions as for pleasure or artistic reasons – a reflection perhaps of the power disjunction between the genders. During the Peninsular War against Napoleon (1808-14), for example, British soldiers reported that Spanish female "guerrillas" were going into battle against the French occupiers (Craddick-Adams: 2005). Historian Isobel Rae also wrote of Dr. James Barry (1796-1865), a qualified regimental surgeon who worked in South Africa, Mauritius, the West Indies, the Crimea, Canada, and Malta (Craddick-Adams: 2005). Barry was only discovered to be female on his deathbed. Dr. Michael Du Preez took an interest in Barry's story and used letters and documents to identify James Barry as one Margaret Ann Bulkley. Du Preez believed the reason for Barry's disguise was so that (s)he could attend medical school, a privilege that was only afforded to males at the time. (Neisel and Herzog: 2007)

Barry cross-dressed to transcend the boundaries imposed upon women at the time; female-to-male cross-dressing was, however, also seen in leisure and pleasure pursuits. According to Stryker and Whittle, transvestism continued to "emerge culturally throughout Europe" at this time (2006:215). This can be seen in celebrations such as public holidays, religious and non-religious rituals, masquerade balls, carnivals and in performance; and at the theatre and the opera (Stryker and Whittle: 2006:215).

Cross-Dressing in the Modern Period: The Twentieth Century

In the 1920s ideas of androgyny were popular with early feminists. Loyo describes this "appropriation of androgyny" as being symbolic of the "new woman" (Loyo: 1996). In 1920s Paris, artists, bohemians, and aristocrats such as Romaine Brooks, Una Tourbridge and the Duchesse de

Clermont-Tonnerre were seen to wear masculine clothing. Garber believes that Brooks's portraits of these women offer one of the "best visual icons of transvestite high style in the period:" "The tuxedo, the cigarette, the cropped haircut, and the monocle are the most recognisable and readable signs of the lesbian culture in Paris." (Garber: 1992:153) Their "look" has been described by Garber as an extension of the style of the "male dandy." (Garber: 1992) This choice of clothing reflected the wearer's social class in more ways than one. Female-to-male cross-dressing was illegal, so upper class women could avoid prosecution by traveling privately, dressed in their male attire. Middle and lower class women, however, were forced to disguise the fact they were cross-dressing by covering themselves in wraps or by traveling under the cover of darkness (Garber: 1992).

In the 1930s, the German actress Marlene Dietrich (1901-92) performed as a nightclub singer in the film *Morocco* (1930), dressed in what Garber describes as, "Dietrich's signature costume of top hat and tails." (Garber: 1991:646) This "costume" led to Dietrich impersonators who would imitate the style in drag. Actresses such as Dietrich and Greta Garbo, who were seen to wear men's clothing, led to the proliferation of women wearing menswear. Garber describes menswear as being "re-sexualised" by these actresses. They were key in the transition from 1920s androgynous styles, worn by the women in Paris, associated with lesbian culture to a "look" associated with straight and gay high fashion.[6]

---

[6] This may have had two aspects: (1) it may have been attractive to women as a way of escaping gender confined roles and of experiencing the freedom of the "other sex;" and (2) it may have been attractive for men who were unconsciously homosexual and attracted to women who look like men.

According to Garber, there have been "dozens if not hundreds" of cases in which cross-dressers have concealed their true gender until their deaths. (Garber: 1992) A more recent example, which received a great deal of media attention, was that of the jazz musician Billy Tipton (1914-89). Tipton, who was formerly known as Dorothy Tipton, was married to a woman, Kitty Oakes, and had three adopted sons. They were all apparently unaware that Tipton was actually a woman. Garber notes that Kitty is said to have been unaware that Tipton was female, because he claimed to have "suffered an injury which required the wearing of broad surgical bandages across the middle of his body for support." (1992:68) Carroll believes that Tipton first began to dress as a man in 1934 to succeed in the music business: "Tipton had been having trouble being taken seriously as a musician and felt that if she were a man, she would have more opportunities to prove herself." (Carroll: 2009:102)

This illustrates the way in which women cross-dressed in order to improve limited career prospects in a society that made it difficult for women to succeed in some jobs; for Tipton it was being taken seriously in the music industry. There are, however, others that believe that Tipton's cross-dressing was not just for professional reasons. Carroll claims that there are many that believe that Tipton was genuinely unhappy being a woman (Carroll: 2009), but such a reason was too shameful for Tipton's wife to admit to at that time.

Transsexuals, Drag Kings, and Club Kids

As the twentieth century continued, technological, medical, and cultural changes have enabled many developments in transsexual, transvestite, and gay culture. In 1931, for example, Lili Elbe was known to be the first transsexual to have the operation to change sex from male-to-female. Ekins (1996) notes that by the 1950s the idea of "sex-changing" was becoming widely known: "Around 1950, the idea of sex-change begins to dominate the literature. A new term 'transsexual,' emerges to distinguish those seeking such a change from other transvestites and, intertwined with the spectacular reporting of some cases in the media, medical reports in English begin to delineate the boundaries of this new category." (Ekins: 1996:86) It was also during the 1950s that the first oral contraceptive pill for women became readily available (Milsom: 2006). This resulted in women having more control over their lifestyle choices, as they were now far less susceptible to unwanted pregnancy. During the 1950s and most of the 1960s, however, it remained illegal to be homosexual in many countries, and those who displayed openly homosexual behavior risked arrest, criminal charges, and other forms of persecution. There was, nonetheless, an active but underground gay culture. Bedell (2007) characterises the atmosphere of the time: "Homosexuality was illegal and hundreds of thousands of men feared being picked up by zealous police wanting easy convictions, often for doing nothing more than looking a bit gay." (Bedell: 2007)

By 1967, a bill to decriminalize homosexuality had been passed in the United Kingdom. Throughout the decade, however, tensions increased both there and in the United States, and in 1969, in New York, the Stonewall Riots spawned what we know today as the modern LGBTQ rights movement (Smith: 2003). In Warren Allen Smith's account of the riots, he recalls that it was a common myth that the drag queens "started it." He claims that the myth is untrue as, "you could not be in full drag at the time." Men were required to be wearing a minimum of three articles of men's clothing; otherwise they would be arrested for impersonating a woman. Smith describes the style worn by what he calls "Flame queens:" "A Flame Queen wore hip huggers, Tom Jones shirts and maybe eye makeup. They would tease up their hair and were very effeminate ... Most young people's clothes at the time had become pretty asexual." (Smith: 2003)

During the 1970s, androgynous styles became very popular with pop stars, notably David Bowie. Sociologist Dick Hebdige believes that Bowie set up a number of historical and visual precedents; these come in the form of the use of androgynous clothing, dyed hair, and makeup (for both men and women). Hebdige believes that Bowie created a 'new sexually ambiguous image for those youngsters willing and brave enough to challenge the notoriously pedestrian stereotypes conventionally available to working-class men and women." (Hebdige: 1979:60)

The emergence of the drag queen subculture and its adoption by the wider culture from the 1950s and 1960s is well known, but by the mid-1980s the first major publicized examples of "drag kings" also emerged. Gelder describes the drag king as counterpart to the drag queen but separate from the "butch lesbian." (Gelder: 2007:57) There are several different types of drag king who "perform" masculinity in different ways, but this has been relatively neglected by both academics and the media. It is, therefore, dealt with in more detail in a separate section below. It is important to note, however, that by the 1990s drag kings had become a "subcultural phenomenon" with regular events in London, New York, and San Francisco. (Halberstam: 2005) At the same time, in New York, the "club kid" subculture was dominating the nightclubs of the city, in particular the notorious nightclub, *Limelight*, where "the group dressed in wildly outrageous and androgynous costumes, experimented with a number of drugs, and promoted hedonistic philosophies of life." (Ott and Mack: 2009:126)

The club kid subculture began to decline when Michael Alig, who was said to be the "king of the club kids," (Ott and Mack: 2009) was charged with the murder of Angel Melendez, Alig's drug dealer, who distinctively wore angel wings (Sullivan: 1997). Alig's story spurred his best friend and fellow club kid, James St. James, to publish his memoirs, *Disco Bloodbath: A Fabulous but True Tale of Murder in Clubland* (1999), which inspired the feature film *Party Monster*, released in 2003.

Cross-dressing, Gender Confusion and Popular Culture

In contemporary culture, we see a broad range of examples that show different elements of cross-dressing. From Christmas pantomimes, which traditionally cast a female to play the male lead, to celebrity "dames" such as Dame Edna Everage (comedian, Barry Humphries), who have achieved global fame. The contemporary media is also full of signs of transvestism. Since the 1950s, there have been numerous filmic representations of cross-dressed characters, in successful films such as *Some Like it Hot* (1959), *Cabaret* (1972), *The Rocky Horror Picture Show* (1975), *Tootsie* (1982), *Mrs. Doubtfire* (1993), and *The Adventures of Priscilla, Queen of the Desert* (1994). Television series also document how widespread transvestism is in the present day. *Ugly Betty* (2006-2010) featured a male-to-female, transgendered character, Alexis Meade, and British television soaps such as *Hollyoaks* and *Coronation Street* have recently featured storylines about gender-confused or cross-dressing characters. *RuPaul's Drag Race* (2008-present) is a reality television series that offers male contestants the opportunity to compete to become "America's next drag superstar" under the guidance of the celebrity drag queen RuPaul.

Although the focus of this research is upon cross-dressing and transvestism within Western culture, it is important to note that attitudes towards cross-dressing in other cultures can be very different. In some ways Western society is reserved in its attitudes towards transvestism in comparison to some other cultures. In India, for example, *Hijras*[7] play an important role within Indian spirituality and are an accepted part of society. (Suthrell: 2004) In Thailand "lady-boys" are an accepted and celebrated part of Thai culture. The Miss Tiffany Universe beauty contest, for example, is a televised beauty competition exclusively for Thai transsexuals. Many of the competition's previous winners have gone on to become pop stars, celebrities, and television hosts. Although we are used to seeing men in drag in the West, the lady-boy television presenters are not chosen for their comedic value, but for their public appeal. As in the West, however, attitudes toward cross-dressing are complex and may include demonization, rejection, and exploitation, as well as acceptance or mere toleration.

---

[7] Hijra means "eunuch" or "hermaphrodite." Hijras are born into a male body but have a female gender identity. They dress in female garments and undertake female roles within society. Hijras have a long recognized history and are spiritually respected by many in India; however, they often work as prostitutes to earn a living.

Blending and Bending: Cross-Dressing and Androgyny in a "Postmodern" World

Introduction

Social and technological developments in the latter part of the twentieth and early twenty-first centuries have had an enormous effect upon the way in which we consider transvestism and on how transvestism exists in Western culture. The post-feminist movement, for example, challenged the beliefs of feminists of the 1970s and the way we think about gender. "Post-feminism," while continuing to pursue feminist agendas around, for example, gender equality, promoted the idea that it was acceptable for women to, if they wished, choose to be a full-time parent and adopt some of the previously rejected characteristics of femininity.[8] One of the key reasons for the decline of the 1970s feminist movement was the concept of "difference" that derived from postmodernism. There were, according to Barrett, some black and ethnic minority women who argued that the feminist movement spoke from a "white experience that was taken – illegitimately – to be universal" in that "differences of social class, age and sexual choice were important too." (Barrett: 2000:48) This postmodernist way of thinking has led to a view of society that is more

---

[8] Post-feminism caused conflict with feminism as feminists saw their ideas as male exploitation in a new guise.

accepting of alternative identities that exist outside of modernist categories. According to postmodernism it is, for example, possible for a person to be an African-American-Jewish-bisexual-woman. Attitudes towards transvestites and, to some extent, transsexuals were also radically affected by the gay rights movement of the 1960s.[9] At the beginning of the twentieth century, being a transvestite would have attracted a great deal of stigma, but today it is more widely accepted and transvestites are less inclined to "hide" in fear of legal or social persecution.[10] They are still, however, subject to the transvestite equivalent of homophobia as prejudices still run deep.

Technologically, developments in cosmetic surgery have changed the way that the human body and its limitations are understood. The use of plastic surgery to enhance or change the body has, as the popular television series *Nip/Tuck* testifies, become widely accepted within Western society as a means of improving what we are "unhappy" with in terms of our bodies or as a means of defying the aging process. While Sexual Reassignment Surgery (SRS) was a fairly new concept during the 1950s, today it is more widely known and performed. The introductory section outlined how the idea of the binary separation of genders is more fluid than it might seem. In contemporary society there is some acceptance of this idea in the form, for example, of ideas about alternative genders or a "third sex." In India, for example, there is the option for Hijras to have the letter "E," for "Eunuch," on their passports rather than "M," for Male

---

[9] Transvestites are often banded together with the gay culture, however, many transvestites are actually heterosexual and married. This can cause tensions, as transvestites may not wish to be regarded as homosexual and some members of the gay community are not accepting of transvestites.

[10] While transvestites have benefitted from the gay rights movement, there are still some social situations and places in which transvestism faces challenges.

or "F," for Female. The expansion of the internet and its presence in almost every aspect of everyday life has also affected the way in which people, across the globe, are able to communicate and create their own realities. New communities and identities have been created which depend upon commonalities and differences of identity across the globe. Hyperreality[11] in cyberspace offers the opportunity to assume a cyber identity, play out a role, or fantasy that is not possible in the "real" world. Transvestites consequently are able to contact other like-minded individuals, research events and clubs and avoid the possibility of embarrassment or exposure by purchasing garments discreetly from an online store. The internet provides instant access to a wealth of information and imagery that supports alternative gender identities. Websites such as YouTube offer tuition and guidance in how to achieve a new "look" using video demonstrations, and individual blogs provide insiders' knowledge and experience of transvestism. This type of information was hidden or only available via membership in private clubs and societies prior to the emergence of the net.

Medicalization of Transvestism

Post war attitudes towards transvestism were not as liberal as they are in contemporary culture. Attitudes in the social and medical realms, as Garber notes, were - and frequently still are – at odds with the desires and beliefs of transvestites. (Garber: 2007) During the 1950s and 1960s, the prevalent model was to treat transvestism and transgenderism [12] as

---

[11] Hyperreality in the context of technology is a means to illustrate the way that our consciousness defines what is "real."

[12] Although the focus here is primarily upon transvestism, transgenderism became a pathway for some (but not all) transvestites who wanted to change their sex. Transvestites are often confused or banded with the transgendered medically and

"problems." Technologies such as Sexual Reassignment Surgery (SRS) and hormone therapies were available; doctors tended to "treat" transvestites medically, as they believed cross-dressing to be a disease or psychiatric disorder (Gagarina: 2011). Ekins describes the treatment prescribed to a 17-year-old male patient who wanted to be female in 1953: "The doctors described him as a 'constitutional homosexual who says he wants to become a woman.' He was treated with male hormones and ECT." (Ekins: 1996, 88) ECT (electroconvulsive therapy) is defined by Kuper and Kuper as an "induction of a cerebral seizure by application of an electrical stimulus to the scalp." (Kuper and Kuper: 1985: 242) The procedure was used to treat psychiatric patients and had some extreme "adverse side-effects" such as memory loss, and fractured and dislocated bones in the patient's body, due to the convulsions caused by the therapy (Kuper and Kuper: 1985).

Many of these therapies were not only subject to extreme side effects but took place in an environment of fear and demonization of transvestites and transgendered individuals, making their "treatment" sometimes appear closer to punishment. Singer captures this when she suggests that the term "transsexuality" was commonly used in the 1950s, to "regulate non-normative gender identities." (Singer: 2006:614) Since the 1990s, however, the umbrella term "transgender" has been used by practitioners to, as Singer notes, "counter the discourse of medical pathologization." Today the umbrella term used by the NHS in the UK is simply "Trans." (NHS: 2011) The NHS now offers a range of treatments

---

socially. Although transsexuals wish to become the opposite gender this is not true of most transvestites. This can sometimes be misinterpreted by an outsider.

to those that it refers to as having "gender dysphoria,"[13] ranging from hormone treatment to peer and relative support groups.

The diversity in treatments implies that there is a greater understanding of alternative identities within contemporary society, but that there are still major differences between the medical and trans models. To some extent these two models exist alongside each other and may offer conflicting and contradictory alternatives for transvestites.

Treatments such as ECT illustrate how, in the late twentieth century, transvestites were demonized in society. They were viewed as socially deviant and treated medically as a "problem." Today there is a greater range of "treatments" available to those wishing to express alternative gender identities. The term "treatment" in itself, however, implies that there is still something "wrong." Although there is a greater acceptance of transvestites in twenty-first century medicine, alongside the acceptance there is still prejudice and many transvestites still live in "fear and loathing."

Contemporary Developments

There have been a number of major developments during the contemporary period. First, bisexuality has become a recognized sexual identity. In recent years the term "bisexual" has become widely recognized in Western culture as a third sexual identity alongside heterosexual and homosexual. This implies that there is a greater acceptance and scope for non-conforming identities to exist. Clarke *et al.* describe bisexuality as transcending the traditional discourse of sexuality: "bisexuality signals a

---

[13] Gender dysphoria is the medical diagnosis given to those who experience discontent with their biological sex.

commitment to moving beyond narrow binary categories of gender and sexuality." (Clarke *et al.*: 2010:87). In 2004, *The Observer* reported a wave of "bisexual chic" in an article that claimed that it is now considered fashionable for young girls in the USA to identify themselves as bisexual: "Emboldened by such images as Madonna kissing Britney Spears and Christina Aguilera on a TV awards show, girls are proudly declaring their alternative sexualities at a younger age than ever before" (Luscombe: 2004).

Second, the way in which we consider the human body has changed. Medical and technical developments have made it possible to transform the body in ways which were previously unimaginable. The proliferation of plastic surgery and quality of cosmetics available over-the-counter allow the individual to present different "selves." In contemporary culture it is viewed as acceptable to modify the "natural" body to enable the individual to show a true identity: "Both the natural body and its depiction can be altered and manipulated; the mixed emotions surrounding such imagery confuse the messages sent and received." (Arnold: 2001:81) The fascination that society has with the body is reflected, as noted above, in popular culture with television series such as *Nip/Tuck* that are centered around plastic surgery, as well as in the more avant-garde statements of artists such as Marc Quinn who, in 2010, exhibited his most recent set of sculptures that feature "people who have defined their body, using plastic surgery and hormones, to turn it into something that reflects their inner self."

As well as celebrities famed for their modified bodies, such as Michael Jackson and Pamela Anderson, Quinn has worked with models Allanah Starr and Buck Angel, who have changed their respective sexes (male-to-female and female-to-male). Rather than using the sculptures for shock value, Quinn believes that his models' bodies document contemporary society: "if you left them in the desert and somebody found them in 5,000 years, it would probably tell them something about the society we live in now … Buck's genes say he should be a girl, but he's decided he doesn't want to be one. It's culture triumphing over biology." (Quinn: 2010)

Blending and Crossover in the Mainstream

Ideas of what constituted femininity and masculinity changed during the late twentieth and early twenty-first centuries and the distinction between gender identities blurred. Recently, it has become popular for males to groom themselves in a much more female manner; this includes eyebrow shaping, tanning, waxing, and even treatment such as Botox are relatively common for men. Male celebrity Simon Cowell openly admits to having had Botox and notes that it has become commonplace in the cosmopolitan space of the city: "Yes, I've had Botox, but not in an obsessive way. Every guy I know who works in the City has had it; it's no more unusual than toothpaste." (Cowell: 2009)

During the 1960s, there was a fashion for unisex clothing. Designers were inspired by the revelations of science fiction and space exploration at the time, which envisioned synthetic jumpsuits that were worn by both men and women. The unisex trend was also reflected more indirectly in the blue jeans and denim shirts worn at the time. Although these styles were designed for both men and women, they tended to reflect aspects of masculinity such as the trouser in their design, so they were not truly "sex-less." (Steele: 2010) In contemporary society, it is now not viewed as abnormal for women or men to wear clothes that were designed for the opposite sex. Catherine Sanchez is the owner and creative mind behind the Ibiza boutique, *reVolver*; on her blog, *White Ibiza,* she writes that customers are much more comfortable buying clothes that might be designed for the opposite gender:

> People often come in, pick something up and ask me if it's for men or women. My answer is always 'yes!' This is Ibiza after all. Some people are a bit taken aback, but in general the Ibiza crowd is more interested in whether they like something and whether it suits them, rather than which side of the shop it's hanging in. (Sanchez: 2010).

Social anxieties over the blending of genders do, however, still exist. Showalter illustrates the way in which social anxieties over gender distinctions might be aroused in relation to the financial, political or cultural climate of the time:

> In periods of cultural insecurity, when there are fears of regression and degeneration, the longing for strict border controls around the definition of gender, as well as race, class, and nationality, becomes especially intense" (Showalter: 1992:4).

Ideas about masculinity and femininity are deep-rooted in our culture; they are part of the "norm," in fact, in Western culture. In deviating from what is for some still a rigid and normative idea of masculinity, transvestites can create social "unease" (Arnold: 2001), anxiety, and even hostility. Despite the greater degree of acceptance in high art and popular culture transvestites may be seen, on the one hand, as "gender outlaws," but, on the other, stigmatised as outsiders or perverts.

Subcultural Theory and Postmodernism

Transvestites can be understood through the separate lenses of subcultural theory and postmodernism. Subcultures are defined by a wide range of social and cultural signs including, for example, music, dance, argot, and demeanor. During the 1950s, youth groups such the rockers, mods, and teddy boys were viewed as "working-class subcultures." (Cohen: 1980). The subcultures of this time were defined by modernists in relation to the class structure. Postmodernists, however, argue that the class basis for subcultural change has disappeared in the contemporary period. Rheingold, for example, talks about the "virtual community," a contemporary subculture made up of those who might be alienated from "modern society" but recover a sense of community on the internet. (Rheingold: 1994) Crane believes that during the 1970s, new subcultural themes surfaced such as "gender subversion and science fiction" (Crane: 2000), which differ markedly from the youth subcultures of the 1950s, 1960s and 1970s. Followers of glam rock and David Bowie in the 1970s began to challenge the established boundaries of gender. According to Hebdige, Bowie was responsible for "opening up questions of sexual identity which had previously been repressed, ignored or merely hinted at in rock and youth culture." (Hebdige: 1979:16) Bowie has also been described as the first singer to "project a blatantly transvestite image." (Crane: 2000)

Postmodernism has brought about a marked shift in our view of subcultures and cultural identities. Identities characteristic of the modern era - which were based around the fundamental categories of class, community, gender, and ethnicity – have given way to a much more diverse set of identities, which either combine elements from previously separate identities or constitute wholly new identities based on the emergence of virtual reality. Postmodernism suggests, therefore, that there is far more cultural "difference" and more social and cultural choice in terms of how we approach and construct our identities; identity itself is, therefore, no longer stable. Perrone, for example, believes that the 1990s "club kids" subculture broke away from "the traditional Hebdige sense of the term" and altered our understanding of youth subcultures. They do not react against the dominant class but rather formed by following the values and "norms" of a newly emerging commodity-based society: "in a society of excessive consumption and commercialism people amplify the value of consumerism, and the use and ownership of goods stand as 'markers of self-identity'" (Perrone: 2007:63). The identities of the club kids were constructed via conspicuous consumption. In the case of transvestites, material culture is used to create a personal style, which transcends, as Suthrell claims, "both sex and gender boundaries." (Suthrell: 2004)

Style and appearance are said to be among the most important elements of subcultural identity (Clarke: 1976). Anticipating to some extent the ideas of postmodernism in the 1970s, Hebdige described style as a process of *bricolage* – by which the individual takes elements from other cultures and identities and creates new meanings from them. (Hebdige: 1979) The clothes worn by a person allow the wearer to create the image or identity that he or she wants to portray to the viewer. Postmodernists, however, characterize the individual by using multiple and complex identities; image may, therefore, be variable in terms of context or social situation. We are, as Suthrell notes, accustomed to the dress codes required for "certain situations:" "Clothes enable a person to look like an executive during the week and a rave-goer at weekends – and the two sets of clothes are seldom interchangeable." (Suthrell: 2004:17). Although interest in unisex clothing and androgyny has grown enormously in the contemporary period (Garber: 1992), historically, the clothing we wear has been loaded with strong gender associations. In creating personal styles, we are "playing," either temporarily or permanently with our identity. (Suthrell: 2004)

Drag Kings and Queens:
Male-to-Female and Female-to-Male Cross-Dressing

Introduction

The final section focuses on transvestism in the form of female-to-male ("drag kings") and male-to-female ("drag queens") cross-dressing and the way in which these roles and practices have changed in contemporary society. Clearly, male-to-female cross-dressing has a much higher cultural profile than its opposite, but has also been changing lately, with drama series such as *Tipping the Velvet* (2002) exemplifying the growing interest in female-to-male transvestism.

Female-to-Male Transvestism

Transvestism is viewed as a "largely male phenomenon" (Garber: 2002). Male transvestism has been discussed by academics at length and often features in popular culture, whereas female transvestism has received some attention, but is not as widely known. Kuzniar (1996) claims that historical case studies show more standout examples of females cross-dressing in comparison to male-to-female examples. This is because female-to-male transvestism is less common and therefore attracts more attention in the contemporary period when instances are highlighted by the media in the case, for example, of Billy Tipton. Female transvestites have, however, recently been much more highly represented in popular culture. Filmic representations such as *Sahara* (1983) and *Salt* (2010) have featured cross-dressed female leads.

In relation to the stigma that has been attached to male transvestism, female transvestites have been afforded some degree of tolerance, and in most cases attracted little more hostility than (patronizing) amusement from society. [14] During the 1930s, however, female lesbians and transvestites caused "moral panics." Radcliffe Hall, a lesbian who lived as a male with a "wife," faced much social stigmatization after her novel, *The Well of Loneliness* (1928), was denounced as "obscene" due to its lesbian content. While instances of male-to-female transvestism are often associated with fetish behavior or personal fantasy (Garber: 2002), female-to-male transvestism is often regarded as separate from eroticism. Kuzniar believes that one of the reasons why a woman might cross-dress is to appropriate some of the power that "comes with male identity." (Kuzniar: 1996) This power might manifest in the form of travel, in times when it was difficult for women to travel alone, or in ways that enabled them to work in or adopt roles only permitted to men: as, for example, "buccaneers, soldiers, doctors, or refugees from the law." (Suthrell: 2004)

Female transvestites have, however, faced difficulty in constructing their own personal styles. While male transvestites have access to female fashion magazines and examples of stereotypical female figures, such as actresses and pop stars, the information available for female transvestites is far less copious. Female transvestites experience different social difficulties from male transvestites. While male

---

[14] This might be a result of the class and status of the female cross-dressers. The 1920s female transvestites, for example, tended to be upper-class and known figures among society and would, therefore, be less likely to face persecution.

transvestites may find community with other male transvestites or female companionship or group affiliation in clubs, female transvestites often experience lonely existences:

> The pamphlet *Information for the Female-to-Male Crossdresser and Transsexual* notes the 'lack of a crossgender peer group' for female-to-males ... males-to-females are interested in 'sisterhood' and 'sorority,' female-to-males lack a sense of community and are often forced to go it alone, reinforcing the stereotype of the strong independent man. (Garber: 2002:51).

"Drag kings," however, are a subculture of female transvestites that tend to exist as a part of performative troupes or groups. "Drag kings" first became noticeable as a subculture in the clubs of New York during the 1980s. While drag queen shows rely upon camp and an exaggeration of femininity, the performance of drag kings is more complex, as masculinity tends to be "nonperformative." (Garber: 1998) Judith Halberstam, an expert in the area of gender studies, has carried out original research on the idea of female masculinity; she is also one of the few people to have observed the drag king culture in depth and over time. Halberstam's research is used as a key reference point in this study.

Drag Kings

The drag king is a strong example of a relatively new subculture that uses style to express personal identity as well as for purposes of performance – the two are often interchangeable. Halberstam defines a drag king as "a female (usually) who dresses up in recognisably male costume and performs theatrically in that costume." (Halberstam: 1998) Diane Torr is a drag king, famous for being one of the first drag kings to pioneer during the 1980s. She is known for her male alter egos, which include Danny King, a personality based upon the middle-class, macho male, who takes elements from men that Torr has known, including her father and Jack Sprat, a cockney singer and former mod. (Torr: 2002) Torr was originally from Scotland, but moved to New York where she became the creator of the *Man for a day/drag king* workshop, a ten-hour event offering an individual makeover, which includes treatment of facial hair and "5 o'clock shadow." Torr asks her students to bring their own men's clothes "for their male identity" as well as hair gel and a "wide elasticated bandage (5 inches minimum) to bind breasts, and a fake penis - (condom stuffed with cotton wool for example)." During the workshop Torr teaches the applicants masculine behavior such as the art of "taking up space," and how to walk, eat, drink, pick up objects and smile as a man in public. (Torr: 2011) On her website, Torr claims that her workshop offers an opportunity to "escape for one day from the social construction of a "woman." (Torr: 2011) The workshops run in numerous cities in America, as well as Europe and Asia.

Some of the key elements involved in drag king style are false facial hair, thickened eyebrows, and a contoured facial structure (often achieved with makeup). There are tutorial videos on YouTube that instruct novices on how to "masculinize the face." The style of clothes and the type of performance given by a drag king is, however, variable. In Halberstam's study of the drag king subculture in performances in nightclubs and competitions in the USA, in New York clubs such as Hershe Bar and Club Casanova. She draws comparisons between the type of drag king found in "drag king competitions" and the drag king who performs in a nightclub. In particular, the drag king competitions, in contrast to the solo and group performances "paid cash prizes and often attracted non-white and non-middle class audiences and participants." (Halberstam: 1998:406) Halberstam suggests that there was a "notable lack of theatricality and camp" in the performances, which depended upon "notions of masculine authenticity," implying that the performer was attempting to pass as an authentic male rather than being read as an impersonator of masculinity. This, as we will see below, is an important differentiating factor in terms of those cross-dressers who may or may not want to pass as the other gender. Beyond this, as noted, there are those who want to move beyond the limitations of both genders. In comparing the drag king contests with similar performances in clubs Halberstam concluded that the Hershe Bar contests and Club Casanova shows displayed "very different forms of drag king culture" but also noted "multiple sites of intersection and overlap between the kings who participated in the contests and the kings who perform in the clubs." (Halberstam: 1998, 406)

At the 1995-1996 Hershe Bar drag contest, Halberstam recalls that the contest attracted a large number of black and Latino competitors, and that the drag kings "flexed and posed" to produce a "spectacle of masculinity." Halberstam noted that the event was a success in terms of displaying alternative masculinities, but found the performance to be a "let down." Halberstam believes this related to the lack of performance within masculinity: "The drag kings had not yet learned how to turn masculinity into theatre … many of the women on stage seemed to be flaunting their own masculinity rather than some theatrical imitation of maleness." (Halberstam: 1998, 408) In the nightclubs, Halberstam claims that there are several subcategories and versions of the drag king within the subculture, including the femme pretender, butch realness, [15] male mimicry, "fag drag," and denaturalised masculinity.

Halberstam defines these categories by the type of performance given by the drag king; a "femme pretender's" performance, for example, is described by Halberstam as "more like drag queen shows" due to the "irony and camp flavor" of the performance: "The femme pretender actually dresses up butch or male only to show how thoroughly her femininity saturates her performance – she performs the failure of her own masculinity as a convincing spectacle." (Halberstam: 2005) Halberstam also explores the idea of "masculinity without men." She describes the "disguise" of the femme pretender that involves exaggerated eyebrows and a goatee beard as being "deliberately overdone" (Halberstam: 1998:249) so that the femme pretender can be read as a woman dressing-up as a man.

"Butch realness" is, as Halberstam describes it, "opposed to femme drag king performances." Those who are in the category of butch realness were often non-white and could easily pass as male. The winner of the Hershe Bar competition falls under this category. Halberstam describes her as a "muscular black woman wearing a basketball shirt and shorts." (Halberstam: 1998, 246)

"Male mimicry" focuses upon an obvious element of masculinity and replicates it, sometimes incorporating irony into the performance. Halberstam identified a "mock priest act" as an example of male mimicry at the contest. Male mimicry can be performed by both butch and femme

---

[15] Butch realness is an example of a convincing/compelling performance of passing by a butch. Here, as in other drag categories, the term realness offsets any implications of inauthenticity within the category (Halberstam: 2005).

according to Halberstam, and it is this type of masculinity that can be seen in Torr's workshops. (Halberstam: 1998)

"Fag drag" is an imitation of stereotypical, gay male masculinity. When describing the fag drag, Halberstam refers to the "Castro clone," which is a "popular masculine aesthetic within urban gay ghettos," such as the Castro district in San Francisco. This style includes leather or denim and is described as a "queer biker" look: "Some of the drag kings in the Hershe Bar contest cultivated a gay male look with leather or handlebar moustaches, and they often routed these looks through a Village People type of performance of hypermasculinity." (Halberstam: 1998, 411)

The final category that Halberstam describes is "denaturalized masculinity." This category can sometimes be misidentified as one of the other categories because it shares elements of butch realness and male mimicry. The example Halberstam uses to characterise denaturalized masculinity is Dred, the winner of the 1996 Hershe Bar contest, with her tribute to "blaxpolitation macho with a butch twist." Halberstam finds her to be an interesting drag king because she "plays the line between the many different versions of drag king theatre:"

> On the one hand, she appears in the bar contest heavily made up as Superfly; on the other hand, she also plays in staged drag king theatrical performances in a much more campy role which she metamorphs [sic] from Superfly to Foxy Brown. Then again, she regularly performs with another drag king, Shon, as part of rap duo Run DMC. (Halberstam: 1998:413)

As Halberstam claims, denaturalized masculinity is similar to but differs from butch realness and male mimicry, because of the theatricality (which is not apparent in butch realness) and by accessing an "alternate mode of the masculine" from male mimicry.

In a performance by Tony Las Vegas, the drag king wore "slicked back hair and a lounge suit" and "performed" sexism and misogyny by making lurid and sexist remarks to the audience. These are the aspects of masculinity most associated with performance. Halberstam believes that by "performing" sexism, drag kings are unmasking the "ideological stakes of male nonperformativity." In playing upon aspects of masculinity most strongly associated with performance, those who perform denaturalized masculinity are often seen to be the most convincing and realistic.

Ekins and King note that male impersonators and drag kings are not necessarily "lesbian roles;" they believe, however, that the butch affect "certainly is." Although cross-dressing women, both on and off stage, are not a new occurrence, many drag king performers have chosen to continue the practice of cross-dressing in their personal lives. Halberstam believes that this is an indicator that the male impersonator's relationship to masculinity "extends far beyond theatricality." (Halberstam: 1998).

Although Halberstam has drawn comparisons between the drag king and drag queen cultures, she stresses that there are vital differences between the two. Femininity in itself is said to be a performance, and as Ekins and King note, drag kings are not merely a female equivalent of a drag queen: "Drag kings are ... a much more subversive phenomenon because of the mainstream view of masculinity as nonperformative." (Ekins and King: 2006:212).

In what follows, the case study of the drag king Amanda Westlake) explores and exemplifies some of these issues.

Case study of a drag king: Interview with Amanda Westlake: August 2011

My research into the drag king subculture led me to Amanda Westlake. Westlake is a member of the Gloucestershire Drag Kings, a drag king troupe, which is based in Gloucestershire in the United Kingdom. She recalls that she always had a fascination with men's clothing, even as a child, and refused to wear skirts or dresses. As she grew older and gained weight, Westlake says she wore men's clothes for comfort and fit. She describes her experience of discovering the drag king subculture as revelatory:

> I hadn't really heard of drag kings before, but 3 years ago I went to Cardiff Pride only to find it had been canceled and a small section of it had moved to a Pulse Street Party, we went to this instead and saw some drag queens, but I had seen flyers for drag kings and was fascinated by them, sadly we didn't get to see them, but it had sparked my interest.

After this event Westlake returned home and used makeup to draw on a moustache and beard. She sent the images to her friends, who responded enthusiastically to the look and urged her to pursue it further. At the time, Westlake had limited knowledge of drag kings and did not know how to become involved in the scene. Unlike Halberstam's New York study, there was a "local" scene that Amanda could key into, but following some encouragement from friends she decided to organize her own charity drag king night. She describes the experience, in terms which are familiar from the oral literature on transvestites, as transformative and addictive, and insists that the event was one of the "most amazing nights ever" for her: "I performed twice, once in a duet with a friend doing '500 miles' by the Proclaimers and then as Elvis doing 'Teddy Bear' and I was hooked."

Westlake labeled her newfound drag king identity as "Ivan Rockenroller." Amanda stresses that although Ivan is a "separate character," he is also at her "inner core." His look is similar to that of a middle-class gentleman, he wears a traditional suit and smart shoes but is influenced by James Dean and Danny Zuko in *Grease*. Using the categories developed by Halberstam, Ivan would come closest to the "male mimicry" category in that (s)he focuses upon relatively obvious elements of masculinity in a way that is sometimes ironic. Unlike Halberstam's drag kings, however, Amanda notes the less glamorous and more practical aspects of cross-dressing in terms, for example, of the problems of paying for and accessing the appropriate clothing to construct Ivan's look:

> Drag kings tend to prefer using waistcoats as this looks smart and is also great at concealing the breasts! I like to look smart and sharp, the only constraint is cost! I could buy so many sharp suits and jackets that I cannot afford! Due to budgets my drag king clothes have mainly come from TK Maxx, Asda, Tesco, and Matalan, etc. The facial hair comes from specialist online shops.

It is worth noting that drag queens are often solo performers, but that drag kings tend to perform as a troupe. Amanda sought to become part of a drag king troupe and made contact with existing UK-based drag kings such as the Manchester Drag Kings and with Valentino King, a famous drag king. This may be in part due to the protection and power that group affiliation can bring. Although comfortable and pleased with her new identity, Amanda has found that she can be misread and misunderstood. Families and close friends are obvious close reference points for transvestites who fear rejection or exclusion from their closest relatives because of their transgressive behavior. Amanda's sister, for example, was concerned that in dressing as a drag king she might be considering a sex-change: "I assured her this was not the case, it was purely a performance for me and a chance to become a new character and to be braver. My mum accepts it, and is politely interested but I don't think she really gets it!"

Although Amanda's experience clearly differs from the experiences outlined in Haberstam's research on New York, it is perhaps more typical of those who find themselves outside of a more developed "scene" and seek to reconcile their differences with the dominant (gendered) culture. It does show similarities with the New York case study, however, in the emphasis it reveals on the revelatory and performative nature of the drag kings, as well as their desire to join together in groups and form communities that may help to insulate them from the prejudices of "outsiders," as well provide a "safe place" and suitable subculture for the exploration of their own identities.

Drag Queens

As noted in the introduction, Western society has, in the past, drawn strong distinctions between men and women who cross-dressed: "Men who both cross-dressed and acted feminine were stigmatized, and their actions were linked with deviant eroticism or, in more modern times, with psychopathology. In this view, such men were "aberrant" (Bullough and Bullough: 1993, 68). The conclusion that follows from this is that one of the generators of Western anxiety over male cross-dressing is the "fear of status loss" in terms of masculinity (Bullough and Bullough: 1993). The traditional idea of the male as the "worker and provider" has been thought to be undermined by transvestism and men who have "blurred definitions of masculinity by expressing an overt interest in fashion" have therefore been "viewed suspiciously within Western culture." (Arnold: 2001) In the 1890s for example, Oscar Wilde was socially persecuted for his acts of homosexuality, flamboyant behavior, and extravagant clothing. Eventually, he was put on trial and jailed for homosexual acts. Suthrell claims, however, that it is unsurprising that at least some men are intrigued and wish to "play" with women's clothing. "The attraction," Suthrell argues, lies in the great "range in terms of colour, style and possibility" compared to men's clothing (Suthrell: 2004).

When we see female-to-male transvestites in film, they are generally given serious, purposeful roles that reinforce the role of masculinity. Angelina Jolie, for example, played a male CIA agent in the film *Salt* (2010). When we see male-to-female transvestites on the screen, however, it is often for comedic purposes as, for example, in the cases of Dustin Hoffman's character in *Tootsie* (1982), Robin Williams's desperate divorced father in *Mrs. Doubtfire* (1994), and the contemporary "camp" comedian Eddie Izzard. Drag queens are an example of male-to-female cross-dressers who are widely known within Western culture and attract diverse audiences. Robert Rodi, the author of the book *Drag Queen*, when interviewed for this research, suggested that, like clowns in the Middle Ages, drag queens serve the social function of reminding society of the "irrational, unpredictable, uncontrollable aspects of natural life;" the things that, Rodi claims, "urban life was constructed to guard against." As he went on to say, "in the same way drag queens are reminders of the artifice of the way we construct sexual identities and categorize sexual desire - which is why some people shun them; they can't take 'hearing" that message'" (Robert Rodi, interview, August 2011).

Halberstam (1998) describes a drag queen as being heavily reliant upon props in performance of femininity; these props include wigs, dresses, makeup, jewelry, and hormones, as well as a suit, facial hair, and crotch stuffers. The drag king's performance, however, is based upon "realism," whereas the drag queen's performance is based around what Gelder describes as an exaggerated form of "the 'stereotyped norms' of femininity." (Gelder: 2007) The impersonation of females by drag queens can, in some circles, be viewed as sexist or insulting in that they can play upon the aforementioned "female stereotypes." Drag queens do not fit neatly into transgender or homosexual stereotypes and are often shunned by these communities:

> (A) large segment of the lesbian and gay population
> frowns on drag queens, who are seen as mocking women,
> all the more so because they get themselves up in the most
> *retardataire* female guises (show girls, prostitutes, sex
> kittens, Hollywood starlets). (White: 1980:191)

Arnold believes that drag highlights the "contradictory nature of fashion:" in one breath it reinforces ideas of femininity but also highlights the fake, in the application of makeup, grooming, and purposeful gestures (Arnold: 2001). In my interview with author Robert Rodi, he also mentioned that the "type" of person who might be a drag queen is somebody who is "deeply interested in the construction of femininity:"

By that I mean, hairstyles, jewelry, fashion, etc. Men who construct a female identity for themselves don't end up presenting themselves as dental hygienists named Betty. They're always glamorous divas named Clytemnestra or something. So it's not so much about having a female identity, as making a comment on the construction of female identity. It's performance art; deeply felt performance art, but performance art all the same. (Robert Rodi, interview, August 2011)

Case Study of a Drag Queen: Interview with William Summers: August 2011

My interview with Will Summers implies that masculinity is central to the performance of at least some drag queens. Will is a 34-year-old drag queen who performs throughout the UK as *Miss Mona Lotte*, but his interview suggests that his main aim is not to be or become to others a "woman:" "I don't like looking like a real woman, I like people to know that there is a man underneath 'a mask.'" For some drag kings (apart Halberstam's "femme pretender"), a close approximation to masculinity is central to the performance. White, however, believes that in the case of drag queens the purpose of drag is not to deceive but is rather an *"art* of impersonation," and he is aware that the drag queen performer in a nightclub is often "careful to reveal his true masculinity" during performance. This could be through the revelation of a flat chest or a masculine, deep voice (White: 1980). Will claims that dressing in feminine clothing is merely a part of his performance and profession; he refers to the clothes he wears as a "costume" but spends time making and designing them. Rather than looking to females for inspiration he looks to existing drag queens on the UK "circuit," which creates a style not necessarily linked to femininity or masculinity but more specific to the drag queen subculture: "I design my own costumes but they are not items that women wear on a day-to-day basis (they are more extravagant)."

Will was brought up in Bargoed, a small town in the Welsh valleys. He describes his community as being "poor" and "working class," but believes that this did not really affect his decision to become a drag queen. He now tours across the UK performing as *Miss Mona Lotte*, but only began to dress in feminine clothing two years prior to our interview, when he became a full-time drag performer. He had, however, always had a personal interest in designing and creating his own clothing. Although he tends to hand-make most of his outfits he will sometimes buy the "odd item of female clothing that catches his eye. His costumes are dresses and range from leopard print and gold sequinned mini dresses to full-length blue PVC dresses. "As for other items, I have my jewelry custom-made and eBay is amazing for stilettoes and tights!" He describes his look as "skinny witty and downright sassy," and believes the key elements of his look are "big wigs and extravagant makeup – something that instantly says I am a drag queen." This is a far cry, then, from the relatively pecuniary nature of Amanda Westlake's cross-dressing, which involved drag king outfits fashioned from clothing available from retailers. The professional drag queen scene involves a much greater and more professionalised input in terms of clothing and styling as well as a much greater outlay in terms of resources. It still, however, encounters difficulties and embarrassments when interfacing with the "straight" community. Will, for example, insists that he is happy with his "career choice," but he finds that he still suffers from embarrassment when buying makeup in public: "When I go to Boots to buy makeup I tend to use the self-service checkouts. I don't know why, but I still get embarrassed in there."

Like Amanda he also believes that those closest to him, his friends and family, accept the fact that he is a drag queen, but he points out that they have never visited any of his live shows and this acceptance may therefore have limits:

> The words 'just so long as you are happy' spring to mind.
> Just so long as I am happy and can afford to pay the rent,

I think my parents are happy with it; my brother didn't even batter [*sic*] an eyelid! Saying that, they have not seen any of my shows! They've only seen photographs and the odd video.

Drag Queens: Culture and Style

The drag queen "scene" varies cross-culturally and within the subculture, but these differences may be more apparent to "insiders." Roberta Perkins' study of the "drag queen scene" in Australia at kings Cross (Sydney) offers an in-depth insight into the drag queen and transsexual subculture in that particular area. In a similar manner to Halberstam, Perkins identifies multiple subcategories among drag queens; the subcategories are, however, based upon the type of role the drag queen plays within the subculture rather than the drag queen's style.[16] Perkins defines these categories as: the showgirls, the strippers, the prostitutes and the girls who pick men up in bars. Perkins believes drag queens to be a singular subculture:

> 'Material artefacts' are the same in all the subgroups. These are the dress and makeup fashions, which are borrowed directly from the wider culture. There is no particular style of dress that is peculiar to either the subgroups or the subculture. (Perkins: 1982:53)

As an insider from the drag queen scene, Rodi claimed that the one clear "dichotomy" that he did find was within the performance scene:

> I noticed it between the drag queens who actually sang their own material, and those who lip synch. The latter don't interest me; they're just playing dress-up. The former, however, are actually fleshing out the persona

---

[16] Although drag queens are not necessarily transgender, all twelve interviewees that Perkins spoke to identify as female.

they've invented—finishing the job, as it were. Letting their own voices be heard. (Rodi: 2011)

While Perkins claims that drag queens borrow their styles from the wider culture, White argues that drag queens borrow their style from female prostitutes and showgirls. White references testimony given to the New York police in 1899 to illustrate his theory: "These men that conduct themselves there – well, they act effeminately; most of them are painted and powdered; they are called Princess this and Lady So and So and the Duchess of Marlboro [*sic*], and get up and sing as women."(White: 1980:191) In contemporary culture it is still commonplace for drag queens to present themselves in such a way.

In my research I have encountered differences that occur generationally and according to location. In an interview with twenty-three year-old cross-dresser and drag queen, Matthew Johnston he claimed that there is a younger generation of drag queens emerging in his town, Stoke-on-Trent, and that they display very different styles to those described by Will Summers and the older generation.

Case Study of a Male Transvestite: Interview with Matthew Johnston

Matthew arguably represents a much more current and challenging form of cross-dressing; one that, in fact, raises the issues of gender-bending and blending but in complex ways. Matthew aspires to be like contemporary glamorous female role models and rejects the styles of earlier "drag queens:"

> I think that Stoke-on-Trent and Blackpool are the only places I can think of that still have a traditional 'drag scene.' It is still very much set in the past, they wear big wigs, big dresses and big makeup. I feel that the younger

generation have seen it and been inspired to bring it forward to 2011. They are inspired by things they see on the television, like *My Big Fat Gypsy Wedding*, and reality shows and this whole new drag scene has taken off!

Matthew describes a sense of "fashion snobbery" between the younger and older generations in the drag scene. He claims that the older generation are not as style- or trend conscious as the younger queens and their makeup looks like "drag makeup," whereas the younger generation aim for a more feminine and realistic look. In his interview, Matthew described an interest in women's fashion at an early age: "I've always liked fashion, in year three, at primary school, we had a fashion show and somebody brought a big box full of clothes in. I was the first person to sign up to model." In later years, Matthew became interested in a career in acting and studied drama. He believes that this, in part, might have something to do with his fascination with dressing up: "The first thing I did was *A Mid-Summer Night's Dream* when I was about 16. I played Theseus in the play. I guess that's where the whole drag idea came from. You have to build a character and there's the magic of the play."

Matthew's first encounters with cross-dressing came about at a party:

Anthony and our mutual friend Craig had cross-dressed for years and one day we were at his house getting ready and they suggested dressing me up. I agreed as I thought it would be fun. Every so often we would come up with a theme as a group, and from that we would make outfits and go out to nightclubs together. We used to make our own outfits to begin with. One year we threw a 'gold' themed party and invited others to join us. We would get ten or eleven guys and girls all dressed up as drag queens! My alter-ego is called Diva/Divaliscious and all she wore was gold, like Foxy Cleopatra in *Austin Powers*, she would wear a big Afro, gold dress, glitter, massive talons, the works.

In a similar manner to Amanda Wakefield, who sought to find a drag king troupe to perform with, Matthew sought group affiliation with his friends but this was only a beginning. Now Matthew is happy to cross-dress without the support of Anthony and Craig:

> Sometimes I'll do it on my own without any of my other friends, Craig has moved away and Anthony is in Ibiza, so I don't really know any other people who do it. I try to tempt some guys I know but it never seems to come to anything, so I just get on with it on my own.

Matthew insisted that much of the personality of his alter-ego, Divaliscious, comes from the choice of wig, and sometimes this personality is unexpected or out of his control. When he bought a red wig that he describes as a red similar to that of "Jessica Rabbit or Satine from Moulin Rouge," Matthew believed that he would be "sultry and sexy;" the personality that "came with the wig," however, was more that of the "entertainer:"

> My choice of wig affects what type of personality I might have on the night. You can be 'you' when you're getting ready, and when you're putting your face on you're still 'you', even when you put that dress on you're still 'you,' but the last thing that goes on is the wig. As soon as that wig hits your head you've got a personality and you don't know what the personality is until that wig touches your head, you don't know - it just comes.

To begin with, Matthew's style was based around the themes selected as a group. But as he became more comfortable and confident as a cross-dresser, he began to look to celebrities for inspiration. He describes his signature look as celebrity inspired and like the "average girl out in Hanley, but 'sluttier.'" He takes inspiration from what he describes as "real'" women like the ultra-feminine girl group, Pussycat Dolls, who wear figure hugging and revealing outfits, to avoid what he describes as the "cartoonish" look of the older generations. Matthew tends to create a look based on an item of clothing or some makeup that stands out to him and he shops in mainstream, high street women's shops such as River Island, Topshop or Quiz:

> I've never bought anything made specifically for cross-dressers or drag queens, like shoes. I crush [my feet] down into a size 8 and get on with it. They look better and the shoes don't wrinkle, they are comfortable too. I stretch them to fit my foot, they don't fall off and they don't look like a 'man dressed in women's shoes.'"

When attempting to appropriate womanly behavior, Matthew looked to television shows such as *America's Next Top Model* and other runway shows and studied how women move and walk in high heels. This and Matthew's fascination with celebrity women is an indication that he is not interested in the "average woman;" he is more interested in the glamorous almost unachievable type of woman that women also try to imitate. While Anthony would apply Matthew's makeup in the beginning, Matthew developed his own personal style: "I learned to put my makeup on from Anthony, he used to do my face. It wasn't very womanly. Anthony likes to be the cartoon, man in drag, whereas I like mine to look natural."

Matthew adopted a similar approach to learning to walk in heels when teaching himself how to apply women's makeup. He uses magazines and the Internet to collect images of celebrities for inspiration:

I'm a bit of a copy-cat, I tend to look to people who have the best makeup. For me Kim Kardasian has the best makeup so I tend to copy her looks from photographs. She's stunning and it's all to do with the makeup, but you have to be so on point. There are other people you could look to like Lady Gaga, but that doesn't really interest me. She's not pretty.

Matthew also relies upon the internet and television shows for inspiration and knowledge. He watches television shows such as *RuPaul's Drag Race* to gain makeup tips and an understanding of how professional drag queens create their looks. He describes RuPaul as "American and flawless:"

Another person that I look to is Roxy Hart, he's a makeup artist and his makeup is brilliant, he specializes in drag and Halloween makeup. I watch him on YouTube. He talks you through the stages from start to finish. They're about twenty minutes long but it usually takes me two and a half to three hours to get my makeup how I want it, whereas the video has been edited down to 20 minutes.

Matthew believes that it is important to perfect the makeup so that outsiders might believe that he is a real woman, but stresses that he has never wanted to be a woman: "That's never crossed my mind, I only do it when the mood takes me." Matthew tends to dress as male within his everyday life and identifies himself as male. Matthew believes that Divaliscious is a part him as far as being a hobby, or an "eccentricity" as he states, however, he believes it is also somebody else:

Once that wig goes on I'm somebody else, you become this person who is ultra-confident, you have to have a drink, otherwise you won't stand a chance. We always have the rule that you don't talk about it on Facebook,

because it's not 'you', we don't tag pictures, because it's
not 'you'!

Matthew believes that his cross-dressing would not have been
possible in his hometown, Worcester, and dresses according to his location
and surroundings:

> My town was not backwards, but it was very prudish and
> conservative. There was nobody interesting. Everybody
> dressed the same. Nobody was allowed to be different. It
> was a very small town of 10,000 people, and the nearest
> city was not much better. As far as I knew, they did not
> have any drag queens or anything similar. When moved
> to Stoke-on-Trent, I found that there were quite a few.

However, even in Stoke-on-Trent Matthew will only travel around
certain 'safe' areas as Divaliscious for fear of victimization and violence:
"I've got quite a boyish frame and figure so I couldn't go out in the middle
of Hanley through 'straightsville' because you will get hit, whereas if you
go to gay bars nobody bats an eyelid."

The interviews with Matthew Johnston and Will Summers imply
that there are still social boundaries within which *Divaliscious* and *Mona
Lotte* can exist. The boundaries are defined in terms of time of day, the
type of venue, and the company which each keeps in a way which points
to the performative aspect of transvestism. As Matthew suggests, he would
not venture into what he calls "straightsville" for fear of getting attacked,
nor would he openly dress in drag around his family for fear of rejection.
It seems, however, that the younger males are taking inspiration from new
media such as the Internet and reality television shows that expose them
to alternative cultures and create a different, more fashion-conscious
image of the cross-dressing male. While Matthew Johnston strives to pass

as a "real woman," Will Summers prefers to create his own identity, one that is not necessarily masculine or feminine. This tendency is even more apparent in the final case study offered here, of Bridge Markland, which illustrates the androgynous tendencies of contemporary cross-dressing.

Case Study of an Androgynous Female: Interview with Bridge Markland

Rather than describing herself as a "cross-dresser," Bridge Markland identifies herself as androgynous. She suggests that androgyny is becoming increasingly common place and socially acceptable as a way of expressing identity in contemporary culture:

> Androgyny comes in waves so to speak, there was a big wave in the 70s, also in the 80s and today. Right now I can see lots of female attributes in males, like plucking of the eyebrows has become very common in straight males, even very muscular ones and masculine ones. Then the very normal looking girls with very long hair suddenly shave one side of their hair as a fashion statement right now. It began when Peaches Geldof did it about two years ago, now I see lots of girls doing it.

Markland is a German performance artist who specializes in "transgendered performances." She has spent 25 years on the stage, and her repertoire includes performances that allow the audience to view a transformation from female-to-male or from male-to-female, cabaret, dance, and biographic and literary-based performances. Alongside Diane Torr, Markland created and curated the Go Drag festival, which focuses upon women performing "male characters." The aim of Go Drag is to "widen gender boundaries and question the ownership of masculinity;" the event features performers from Scandinavia, Italy, Austria, Germany,

Great Britain, and the USA, and is designed to inform and create a cultural impact upon the cities it visits. Media across the globe have described her work as "bizarre," "curious," and "compeling." In one of her acts, "The Most Beautiful Woman in the World," Markland begins as a female character, dressed in a gold sequined dress, with a bright wig. During the performance, Markland removes layers in a striptease manner to reveal a shaved head and tights and an androgynous appearance, before finally adding a new set of layers and presenting herself as a male. In her act, Markland uses props such as wigs, moustaches, neckties, and uniforms, which are familiar to cross-dressers of many stamps. It seems as well that for Markland and Jones the wig plays a large part in defining the character.

In the previous case studies, those involved described an alter-ego that they created for either their performance or for when they dress-up. Markland, however, believes that she keeps the same identity both on and off the stage. "There is no separation between who I am onstage and the person I am in my day to day life. When I go onstage I am not assuming a role, I am telling a story." Markland believes that her appearance and personal style may lead outsiders to question her actual gender. She does not have the appearance of a drag king with telltale, false facial hair, nor does she display the giveaway signs of a woman "dressing up" as a man:

> I dress relatively androgynous in private, because of my shaved head some people perceive me as male. Other people get very confused as they cannot see a clear gender definition in the way I look and dress. Often even when I am dressed as a female with a wig some people think I am male dressing as a girl, even children do.

Living in Berlin, Markland claims that her appearance is widely accepted and unnoticed. However, when on holiday in a village close to

Berlin, Markland recalls that she was "stared at a lot" by the locals. In a similar manner to Matthew Johnston's story, Bridge Markland notes the acceptance of her look where she currently lives (Berlin is widely known for eccentric and unusual street styles), but also the hostility (s)he encounters when venturing outside of her "homelands."

Conclusion

Although gender came to be identified during the twentieth century with the binary opposition of male and female, it is clear from the discussion above that this has not always been the case, nor has it been true in all cultures. Gender is socially and culturally constructed and not, therefore, based on timeless biological differences. The challenging of gender as a fixed category which accompanied the emergence of modern feminism has been superseded by skepticism toward all fixed forms of conceiving of gender and sexuality. In this respect, transvestism has become central to many aspects of contemporary social thought and cultural practice.

As we saw at the beginning of this book, there have always been those who, throughout history, have sought to cross established boundaries between the genders for social, political, economic, political, and cultural reasons. Artists have exploited the ambiguity and confusion that have resulted from such transgressions for both comedic and dramatic purposes. More contemporary performance-based artists have made themselves the subject of gender transformations which have contributed to the more general questioning of gender as a fixed category of identity. While the gay rights movement broke down the barriers to the participation of gay people in the wider society and challenged the demonization of gay relationships, there have been others who, while riding on this wave, have nevertheless felt themselves to be to some extent outside of and beyond it.

At the same time, as we have also seen the confusion, anxiety, and hostility which have accompanied the crossing of boundaries continue to exist despite the apparently more liberal acceptance of gay and transvestite identities. In some (non-Western) parts of the world, expressions of these identities can still attract persecution and imprisonment, while in the West itself homophobia still affects parts of the community. More generally, the existence of groups and individuals exposing transvestite and gay identities causes cultural anxiety and threatens the self-identity of those who hark back to more fundamental social, religious, and cultural forms. To this extent transvestism, although it is increasingly embraced and explored through sub-cultural forms and movements still threatens the assumptions of the wider society. The fact that it transgresses is, in fact, perhaps part of its attraction, although the risks and the punishments it produces may be unwelcome in themselves.

The fashion industry can be argued to both reinforce and challenge contemporary gender stereotypes, even though it is only a small part of a much wider "postmodern" system of cultural industries which produce a proliferation of images and styles. Signs and symbols have, in any case, always faced in many directions and been capable of many interpretations. It is this which contributes, together with the deliberate ambiguity of many forms of "gender bending," to the difficulty of interpreting the precise meaning of many contemporary manifestations of transvestism and transgender experimentation.

Nevertheless, a number of conclusions can be drawn from the above discussion. First, a stronger transvestite movement has emerged, which is linked to but also relatively separate from the wider gay movement. As we have seen, some feminists and gay thinkers have regarded transvestism as a conservative phenomenon to reproduce the most exploitative aspects of female appearance and subordinate behavior. Arguably, however, it has also been regarded by others as liberating to the extent that it has released them from gender stereotypes which have not seemed to apply to their own understanding and experience of gender relations. To this extent, it is important to recognize the wide range of transgendered identities and the possibilities, noted above, of identities which seek to go beyond or transcend the limitations of contemporary gender roles. The range is, as we have seen, very broad: from those who seek to embrace both the behavior and physical form of the other gender to those who conceive of themselves as experimenting with, blending, and bending gender characteristics in order to create new gendered or non-gender identities. In this respect, the Internet has been particularly influential, with cyber identities – allied perhaps to alter   egos – providing opportunities to go outside oneself and explore ideas, fantasies, or unrealised ambitions that are not normally possible in the "real world." Cyber identities and scenarios make it possible to embrace extended versions of (hyper) reality in ways which are now highly sophisticated and challenge the boundaries between the real and the un- or hyper real.

Second, a range of cultural practices have emerged which not only subvert and undermine gender differences as in the past, but try to create mixed or blended identities. This is reflected in fashion through new cross-over and androgynous styles, the adoption by males of female styles and cosmetics, and the feminization of men's fashion. Fashion, as Arnold notes, is always the "product of the culture that spawns it" (Arnold: 2001), and contemporary culture is perhaps, as postmodernists suggest, open to the creation of hybrids and diversity of identity. In the twenty-first century we have seen how the fashion industry been influenced by as well as been an influence on the multiple gender identities available in contemporary society to create captivating imagery or to promote a product based on the "new:"

> Fashion is no longer concerned with producing only images of perfection that smooth out the reality of the body and the harshness of Western capitalist culture. It now encompasses references to death and decay, uncertainty, and yearning, in its allusions to the detritus of the city, illuminating the shifting moralities of contemporary existence. (Arnold: 2001:125)

The contemporary trends of unisex and androgyny reflect the current cultural climate and exemplify how fashion seeks to blur what was once set distinctions between the binary genders.

Finally, the emergence of ideas and practices around the third gender and the transcending of gender barriers – summarized at the outset as the role of new "gender outlaws" - has been pioneered in the arts and subcultures. It is not always clear whether the role of fashion has been to aid or exploit this process, as there are numerous examples, of fashion exploiting the titillation and excitement that derives from transgression. To the extent that the modern fashion industry has had, as its main consumers, women, it has been the female-to-male transformation that has been foregrounded, while the male "drag queen" has been dominant in other sectors of the culture industry such as film and performance. As we have seen, this relatively stereotypical set of relations is starting to break down, albeit in complex and unexpected ways. There is a certain degree of permissiveness that goes with this, although its limitations are all too clear in the face of homophobic responses to any form of sartorial or sexual transgression. There are those, nevertheless, who see themselves as exploring the outer limits of gendered identities, whether this be in the form of style, clothing, or consumption on the one hand, or the artistic and subcultural exploration of the body on the other. Some of those interviewed above exhibit precisely these attributes, often in complex and contradictory ways. The limits are not simply the limits of their (collective) imaginations, but the sometimes more mundane limitations of resources and location as well as the limits set by social relationships which inhibit creativity and experimentation.

Appendices

Appendix A
Transcript of Interview with Amanda Westlake

July 13, 2011

Personal information:

Name: Amanda Westlake

Age: 36

Place of Origin: Cirencester, Gloucestershire, UK

Background information:

Could you summarize your past? (This might include family/friendships/education/ work or anything else you feel might be relevant?)

"I was born to a farming family as one half of a twin, 5 minutes older than my sister, we are non identical twins and as we grew up we started going in our separate directions and are basically chalk and cheese. We grew up in a farming environment and lived and breathed horses and the outdoors. At the age of 14 I started to lose interest and my confidence in horse riding due to a couple of nasty falls. During this time I wanted to socialize and be a "normal teenager" but with family commitments it wasn't possible and I resented this for a while.

I went to an all girls private school, a convent and loved every minute of it, it was a very small personal school and perfect for me, I don't think I would have done very well in a large school!

After school I went to a larger mixed sex 6th Form and I enjoyed the freedom and being around new people and mixing with guys. I had a few casual boyfriends but nothing serious.

After 6th Form I started working at various companies and eventually settled for 6 years at Mitsubishi Motors UK HQ and loved my time there but wanted to get into web design so went to work for a small but vibrant web design company in Cheltenham. I stayed there for 2 years and was made redundant and spent the next year working and temping across Cirencester and the surrounding areas. I then managed to get back into Mitsubishi Motors where I stayed for another 5 years.

During this time I started to question my sexuality and found it easier to hide away and not socialise and spend time with my mum who was also now single. So when she met someone I realised I needed to have my own life, so started looking at lesbian online dating sites, I talked to a few people but was really nervous. I did meet one lady but found the situation too much and disappeared offline for a few months. Eventually I decided to try it again and met (my now best friend) and a fab group of friends and for the first time ever felt I fitted in somewhere. My confidence gained, I had a make-over and actually took care of my appearance rather than hiding behind it.I met my first partner within a few months, which was a complete revelation to me, finally feeling it was ok to love it was ok to love someone, to be loved and enjoy sharing my life. Sadly this wasn't to last and turned into a destructive force for me, one I couldn't walk away from easily and eventually I did.

During this time with my friends I learnt of the old scene in Cheltenham and the gay community and how it had all but disappeared. I felt I was lucky for coming out with the support of a great bunch of friends, so decided to create a social group for the Gay Girls of Gloucestershire. I started having regular meet ups and over the past three years it has grown into a thriving group and I have met the most amazing friends."

When did you become interested in masculine clothing? What attracted you to it?

"As a child my parents never really pushed the whole girly image, sure we had to wear dresses etc and I hated it, whenever I had to wear a dress I would kick up a stink and have a strop! I was much more comfortable in trousers and jeans and t-shirts.

As I got older and also put on weight I found men's clothing actually fitted me better so would wear men's t shirts and hoodies and occasionally jeans."

Were you aware of drag kings at this time?

"I hadn't really heard of drag kings before, but 3 years ago I went to Cardiff Pride only to find it had been canceled and a small section of it had moved to a Pulse Street Party, we went to this instead and saw some drag queens but I had seen flyers for drag kings and was fascinated by them, sadly we didn't get to see them, but it had sparked my interest. I came home and used make up and drew a moustache and beard and sent it to my mates who all said I looked really good and should do it properly. I didn't really know anything about drag kings so didn't pursue it."

How did you get involved with the drag king scene? Was it easy to communicate? How were you received?

"I told a few friends about my penchant for drag kings and that I would love to do it, and was encouraged to give it a go. So I decided to create a charity night as part of the Gay Girls of Gloucestershire Group and make it a drag king night, I asked for people to volunteer to perform as drag kings, either solos, duets or groups. I also asked the audience to dress up as well if they wanted. This was one of the most amazing nights ever! I performed twice, once in a duet with a friend doing 500 miles by the Proclaimers and then as Elvis doing "Teddy Bear" and I was hooked!

After this night I contacted various drag kings (Valentino King & The Manchester Drag Kings) and had a lot of help from Valentino and he was great support. I then decided I wanted to form a troupe of drag kings in Gloucestershire, so put an advert on the GGG group and immediately Lynn got in touch to say she had loved the night so much and wanted to do drag king'ing as well. We then recruited a mutual friend, Emma and a friend of mine Libby came on board. After our first meet up, Leanne decided she couldn't commit to the group and my best friend Sarah then came on board and the Gloucestershire drag kings were born."

Is it something you do in your private life or just for performance?

"I feel that my alter ego, Ivan Rockenroller is a separate character but is part of me, like the inner core. I don't dress up as Ivan apart from when doing a drag king event."

How would you describe your look?

"I would describe Ivan as a smooth, gentle gentleman. A classy traditional man, suited and booted etc. My idols are Elvis, James Dean, Danny from Grease."

Do you find it easy to create your look? (What sort of stores do you shop in? How do the people in the stores react? Any technical difficulties?)

"Yes, the look isn't hard to create, drag kings tend to prefer using waistcoats as this looks smart and is also great at concealing the breasts! I like to look smart and sharp, the only constraint is cost! I could buy so many sharp suits and jackets that I cant afford!

Due to budgets my drag king clothes have mainly come from TK Maxx, Asda, Tesco, Matalan etc. The facial hair etc comes from online shops etc."

How did your family/friends react to you becoming a drag king (positive/negative reactions?)

"My sister found it all very confusing and didn't like me talking about it, eventually I got her to admit that she thought this meant that I would be looking to have a sex change. I assured her this was not the case, it was purely a performance for me and a chance to become a new character and be braver!

My mum accepts it, and is politely interested but I don't think she really gets it!

I was extremely chuffed when my mum and sister turned up to see us perform at Gloucestershire Pride and was happy when they said they enjoyed it and could see they kind of accepted what we did and it wasn't as bad as they had originally thought.

My dad supports me whatever I do really, as long as I don't rub it in his face he is cool.

I think my family still struggle deep down with me being gay, but they are getting there!"

Appendix B
Transcript of Interview with Matthew "Samantha" Johnston

July 15, 2011

Personal information:

Name: Matthew Johnston

Age: 23

Hometown: Worcester, UK

Current location: Stoke-on-Trent, UK

Background

Could you describe your background and upbringing?

"I lived in Worcester until the age of 18-years-old with my mum, dad and two sisters. It was a very happy childhood, nothing dramatic or terrible happened that you might expect with this sort of thing, I'm from a very normal, 2.4 children family."

What were your first memories/experiences of fashion?

"I've always liked fashion, in year three at primary school we had a fashion show at school and somebody brought a big box full of clothes in and I was the first one to sign up to model, because I thought, I want to do this! I did not grow up with anyone particularly glamorous or outlandish in my life. My town wasn't backwards, but it was very prudish and conservative. There's nobody interesting there. Everybody dresses the same, nobody is allowed to be different, it was a very small town of 10,000 people, and the nearest city wasn't much better."

When did you develop an interest in women's fashion:

"In terms of women's clothing I had more of a general interest in it from the fashion perspective, I did a lot of dressing up and acting when I was younger so I suppose it came from that. The first thing I did was *A Mid-Summer Night's Dream* when I was about 16, I played Theseus in the play, I guess that's where the whole drag idea came from. You have to build a character and there's the magic of the play. I then went onto college and did drama as an A-level, when I went to university I studied law and criminology and changed to criminology and marketing, so I took what I thought was going to be a year out and never went back."

What aspects of fashion are you interested in?

"I'm quite interested in high-end style, I love the catwalks I love the drama they bring. There's just the whole idea that there's a piece of art walking in front of you and it's bigger and better and more interesting with every designer that comes out. Sometimes you think that the idea is so simple, how could anyone else have missed it?"

How would you describe your personal style?

"When I dress up I would describe my style as you're average girl in Hanley, but a bit sluttier!! "

When did you begin to cross-dress?

"Anthony and our mutual friend Craig had cross-dressed for years and one day we were at his house getting ready and they suggested dressing me up. I agreed as I thought it would be fun. Every so often we would come up with a theme as a group, and from that we would make outfits and go out to nightclubs together. We used to make our own outfits to begin with. One year we threw a 'gold' themed party and invited others to join us. We would get ten or eleven guys and girls all dressed up as drag queens! My alter-ego is called Diva/Divaliscious and all she wore was gold, like Foxy Cleopatra from Austin Powers, she would wear a big afro, gold dress, glitter, massive talons the works. My style began with this theme then I became more inspired by celebrities, I see an item of clothing and then I want to work around that, I see it and think might wear that then work the rest of the outfit around that. Or I see some makeup and think, "she looks amazing! I'm going to do my makeup like that" and then work the outfit around the face. My style at the moment is very much like the Pussy Cat Dolls, crop-tops, leather, just cheap and nasty but very feminine like a 'real woman'."

Where do you buy your makeup from and how did you learn to apply it?

"I always spend a fortune on eyelashes, makeup, nails and wigs. I shop in River Island, Quiz, I go to the market for my makeup, I'll shop anywhere!I use magazines, the Internet and anything like that to find out about makeup. I'm a bit of a copy-cat, I tend to look to people who have the best makeup, Kim Kardasian has the best makeup so I tend to copy her makeup from photographs. She's stunning and it's all to do with the makeup, but you have to be so on point. There are other people you could look to like Lady Gaga but that doesn't really interest me, I think that's going backwards, it's not pretty as such, it's like a disguise and a bit to out there. I learned to put my makeup on from Anthony; he used to do my face. It wasn't very womanly; Anthony likes to be the 'cartoon', man in drag, whereas I like mine to look natural. I ended up watching *RuPaul's Drag Race*, he's the most famous drag queen if you ask me. He's American and flawless, he has a show where he finds 12 acts from around the USA and they compete in challenges every week and eventually one of them is crowned a winner and gets their own Vegas show. I learned a lot from watching the show and got makeup tips from there. Another person that I look to is Roxy Harton YouTube, he does drag and Halloween makeup he's a makeup artist and his makeup is brilliant. He talks you through the stages from start to finish. They're about twenty minutes long but it usually takes me 2 and a half to 3 hours to get my makeup how I want it, whereas the video has been edited down to 20mins. Largely I use pictures from people on the Internet, especially the eyes, as they're where I fall down, I struggle with the eyes. I find it difficult to use liquid eyeliner so I try to find ways to get around this by looking at what others have done. A big one at the moment is double-winged eyeliner, it's absolutely amazing, and I really like that."

Where do you tend to buy your female outfits from?

"I've never bought anything made specifically for cross-dressers or drag queens, like shoes. I crush down into a size 8 and get on with it. They look better and the shoes don't wrinkle, they're comfortable too. I stretch them to fit my foot, they don't fall off and they don't look like a 'man dressed in women's shoes.' Walking came very naturally, I just put them on and it came naturally, I've watched enough of *Americas Next Top Model* and other runway shows to know how to walk in a pair of massive heels."

Have you ever had any unusual reactions from store staff?

"I've never had any strange reactions. You could be buying for anyone, nobody really knows. You only ever get sussed out when you go to a makeup counter and you know what you're talking about -that's when they guess what you're doing, but there's never been an adverse reaction. I think that's because it's quite common for guys to cross-dress in Stoke-on-Tent."

Do you feel that Divaliscious is a part of you?

"Me and the alter-ego, we're very different, but at the same time it's still me. When I'm a boy I'm me and when I'm a girl I'm somebody else. I like to see people's reactions when I'm out - it's a laugh. The reactions are very different with different people; often people don't actually know it's me when I go out, particularly my friends. Especially as I often change my wigs, makeup, and outfits, people don't realise it's me. It's part of me as far as being a hobby, an eccentricity I suppose, it's not fully a part of me because once that wig goes on I'm somebody else, you become this person that's ultra confident, you have to have a drink, otherwise you won't stand a chance. It depends upon how much you do it and how much you like doing it how bigger part it is."

What would you say the most important factor is when constructing your personal style?

"My choice of wig effects what type of personality I might have you can be you, when you're getting ready when you're putting your face on you're still you, even when you put the dress on but the last thing that goes on is the wig. As soon as that wig hits your head you've got a personality and you don't know what the personality is until that wig touches your head, you don't know it just comes. Like you can see a wig and really like it, buy it put it on and it might not be the wig you were looking for. It's a bit odd but that's how I've always found it. I've got two I mainly use, one is like Jessica rabbit/Satine Moulin Rouge that sort of red, I expected it to go on and be quite sultry and sexy but the personality that comes with it is actually quite silly, you run around fall over, you're very much the entertainer. You're very ditzy, silly, twirling your fingers. My latest one is poker straight, straight dark brown, very dark like Kim K but evil pure evil, people will not talk to you in that wig! They will not come near you because they think you're going to poke their eyes out! I've had a couple of guys coming over and chatting before realising it's me, Matthew."

Do you hope to pass as a woman?

"I think it's important to get your makeup, so perfect that people can believe I'm a real woman. I've never wanted to be a woman, that's never crossed my mind. I only do it when the mood takes me, sometimes I'll be walking through Hanley and it's almost always me and Anthony and we'll see a dress and then we'll decide we want to dress up."

Do you dress up every time you go out or occasionally?

"It's very rare I do it for a specific occasion although I'm doing it as a surprise for my friend's birthday party in a few weeks. I've got quite a boyish frame and figure so I couldn't go out in the middle of Hanley through 'straightsville' because you will get hit, whereas if you go to gay bars nobody bats an eyelid, in Manchester, nobody bats an eyelid."

Would you say it is 'common' in Stoke-on-Trent?

"I've lived somewhere very conservative before and they didn't have any drag queens. I moved to Stoke and then there was quite a few. A lot of professionals and there wasn't anyone that really did it as a joke, now it seems to have taken off a lot of people seem to have started doing it. The older queens are stuck in a rut, they look like men dressed up as women whereas the younger ones like me are more fashion conscious and look more like a real woman. I think Stoke and Blackpool are the only places I can think of that still have this massive 'drag scene'. It's still very much set in the past, big wigs, big dresses, but I feel that the younger generation have seen it and decided to bring it forward to 2011. I don't know why it's more prevalent here, it must be something in the water."

What inspires the 'younger generation' of male transvestites and drag queens?

"People are inspired by things they see on the television, like My Big Fat

Gypsy Wedding, RuPaul's Drag race, and other reality shows and celebrities such as Kimora Lee Simons and Kim Kardashian– it has really taken off.

Do you publicly broadcast the fact that you cross-dress, e.g. on Facebook?

"I don't talk about it on Facebook, because my family don't know and they would worry that I want to change sex. They've already had to deal with the 'gay' thing, they don't need to deal with the 'do you think you're a woman' thing! We always have the rule that you don't talk about it on Facebook because it's not 'you', you don't tag pictures, because it's not 'you'! I don't have photos online because my family are all on there."

How did your friends react to your cross-dressing?

"My friends are that used to me being the way that I am that they wouldn't bat an eyelid anymore, I'm probably going to turn up to this party in two weeks and they probably won't even react to it! I've never had anyone knock me down for it, everyone has been supportive in that they find it funny and I make their evening. It's just something else to add on to their night making it more entertaining instead of being boring. I like to have a giggle and play around. Sometimes I'll do it on my own without any of my other friends, Craig one of the guys who I did it with first has moved away and Anthony is in Ibiza so I don't really know any other people who do it. I try to tempt some guys I know but it never seems to come to anything, so I just get on with it on my own. I think it's funny. I'd definitely have the confidence to go out and do it on my own, of course after a few drinks."

Are you comfortable with your identity?

"It took a long time for me to be comfortable with who I am, coming from where I was from, but now I would probably say that I am the most comfortable out of anyone I've ever met. Living in S-o-T I've never had any sort of homophobic abuse it's very accepting, whereas back home I would get it all the time just for wearing nice clothes. Even straight guys would get it. If you dress nicely you're a 'puff'. Whereas here everyone's very accepting, there's a couple of people I know who are boys who look like girls or transsexuals and people don't bat an eyelid, people don't shout anything in the streets. The atmosphere up here is a lot friendlier and warmer and there's no need for people to live in fear."

Appendix C
Transcript of Interview with Robert Rodi via Skype

August 6, 2011

Personal Information:

Name: Robert Rodi

Place of Origin: Chicago, USA

What interested you about the drag scene?

"Drag seems to me, oddly, a very masculine thing, very testosterone driven. The same hormonal surges that drive men to build bridges and fly to the moon are the same that drive some men to completely re-invent their identities as drag queens. There's no corresponding phenomenon among lesbians; you see very butch dykes, very masculine, true, but it's just the way they are -- it's not an identity they've assumed; it's not something they've achieved through force of will. Butch lesbians don't get that way by watching 800 Gary Cooper movies and slavishly imitating everything he does, but drag queens happily do that with Marlene Dietrich or whoever. So what interested me about drag queens was that paradox, of masculine drive put in the service of constructing a female identity."

Did you find there were any types of subcultures within the drag scene?

"The one dichotomy I found, that I felt strongly about, was on the performance scene: drag queens who actually sang their own material, and those who lip synch. The latter don't interest me; they're just playing dress-up. The former, however, are actually fleshing out the persona they've invented—finishing the job, as it were. Letting their own voices be heard."

Is there a specific type of person who would tend to be a drag queen?

"I suspect it's someone deeply interested in the construction of femininity. By that I mean, hairstyles, jewelry, fashion, etc. Men who construct a female identity for themselves don't end up presenting themselves as dental hygienists named Betty. They're always glamorous divas named Clytemnestra or something. So it's not so much about having a female identity, as making a comment on the construction of female identity. It's performance art; deeply felt performance art, but performance art all the same."

Were there any areas of particular interest to you when preparing your book?

"I was interested in the social role of drag queens. They're sort of like clowns in Middle Ages -- far from pleasant, happy figures, clowns served a social function, by reminding people of the irrational, unpredictable, uncontrollable aspects of natural life -- the things urban life was constructed to guard against. In the same way drag queens are reminders of the artifice of the way we construct sexual identities and categorize sexual desire -- which is why some people shun them; they can't take "hearing" that message."

Appendix D

Transcript for Interview with William Summers (Miss Mona Lotte)

August 6, 2011

Personal information:

Name: Will Summers AKA Miss Mona Lotte

Age:22

Place of Origin: Bargoed, Welsh valleys, UK

Background information:

Could you summarise your past? (This might include family/ friendship/ education/work or anything else you feel might be relevant?)

"I studied in an all boys school in a poor community. I have a tight close-knit family who are very supportive of me. I have had a lot of friendships although a few have ended over silly little things and loyalty. At the moment I have the most amazing partner whom I have been with for four years and without him I don't think id be who I am today."

When did you become interested in feminine clothing? What attracted you to it?

"I was never really wore female clothes until the other year when I decided to take drag as a full time career. Before that I was interested in designing and making both men's and women's clothes. I design my own costumes but they are costumes not items that women wear on a day-to-day basis. They are more extravagant!"

Is it something you do in your private life of just for performance?

"It's purely for performance and purely for making a living … it's a good laugh though! I get enjoyment out of being on stage and performing."

How would you describe your look?

"Big wigs, extravagant make up - something that instantly says I'm a drag queen! I don't like looking like a real woman, I like people to know that there's a man underneath "a mask". I'm very slight and I do have a feminine figure. 'I'm skinny witty and down right sassy!'"

Do you find it easy to create your look? (What sort of stores do you shop in? How do the people in the stores react? Any technical difficulties?

"It depends. I know some drag queens that shop in ladies stores. All my costumes are custom made and designed, although there may be the odd item of female clothing that catches my eye. I have been 'drag shopping' before and it really doesn't bother me what other people think. I've had a few looks but I'm happy with my career choice.

As for other items I have my jewelry custom made and eBay is amazing for stilettoes and tights! Boots is always a laugh when buying makeup although I normally use the self-service. I don't know why, but sometimes I can get embarrassed.

How did your family/friends react to you becoming a drag queen? (positive/negative reactions?)

"The words 'just so long as you are happy' spring to mind. Just so long as I'm happy and can afford to pay the rent I think my parents are happy with it ... My brother didn't even batter an eye lid! Saying that though, they haven't seen any of my shows! (Only photographs and the odd video)."

Appendix E
Transcript of Interview with Leah Timpani (Valentino) via Skype

August 11, 2011

Personal information:

Name: Leah Gezellia Timpani

Age: 43

Place of Origin: Born in Rochdale, UK to an English mother and Italian father

When did you become interested in masculine clothing? What attracted you to it?

"I explored the possibility of impersonating a man a few years ago, purely from a performance point of view."

How did you become involved with the drag scene?

"Whilst looking for additional work, I was asked if I would 'drag up'. My reply was a definite 'yes', even though I had never done this before. I quickly began to think of my new alter ego and how to develop it. Initially it was was difficult to 'sell' the idea to venues as people did not know what a dreg king was, let alone want to book one. Having said that the reaction was fantastic from day one. People are intrigued at the whole concept of a woman impersonating a man, even though vice versa happens all the time."

Where do you preform? Is dressing as a man something you do in your private life of just for performance?

"I perform all around the UK and in Europe. Mostly in gay venues, although I have been booked in mainstream venues from time-to-time. Most of my work is in and around the Manchester area.

This is something that I do purely as part of my work, and does not cross over into my private life. This is not true of all drag kings though I have to say."

How would you describe your look?

"I have many personas but only one alter ego. I do wear many different costumes, from cowboy to LA cop, but have resisted creating a different character for each one. Valentino is quite a clean-cut character with a definite camp side to him."

Do you find it easy to create your look? - What sort of stores do you shop in? How do the people in the stores react?

"I have never had any problems coming up with costumes or indeed buying them. I shop in charity shops, army surplus and online. Sometimes I do suppose I get the odd strange look when purchasing an officer's uniform, but I am used to it now. I tell other kings who are buying for the first time to just pass it off as a fancy dress costume. This usually works for them.

How did your family/friends react to you cross-dressing?

"My family don't get shocked at anything any more. They are so used to me trying different things as part of my work as an entertainer. So becoming a drag king - they really didn't bat an eyelid!

As far as friends go they just think it is thinking outside the box and wish they had thought of the idea."

Bibliography

(2011) *Living my life*, NHS [online] accessed at URL: http://www.nhs.uk/Livewell/Transhealth/Documents/LivingMyLife.pdf last accesed: 21-8-2011

Alkin, L (2005) *Elizabethan Era* [online] accessed at URL: http://www.elizabethan-era.org.uk/ last accessed: 15-8-2011

Arnold, R (2001) *Fashion, Desire and Anxiety Image and Mortality in the 20th Century*, New York, I.B Tauris and Co. Ltd

Barnard, M (2007) *Fashion Theory: A Reader*, UK, Routledge

Barrett, M (2000) cited in Browning, G *et al.* (2000) *Understanding Contemporary Society*. London, Thousand Oaks, New Delhi. Sage Publications

Bedell, G (2007) *Coming out of the dark ages*, The Guardian [online] accessed at URL: http://www.guardian.co.uk/society/2007/jun/24/ communities.gayrights, last accessed: 21-8-2011

Bolich, G (2007) *Conversing on Gender*, USA, Raleigh

Bullough, V. and Bullough B (1993) *Cross-dressing, Sex and Gender* Philadelphia and Pennsylvania, University of Pennsylvania Press

Butler, J and Garber, M (2006) in Ekins, R and king, D (2006) *The Transgender Phenomenon,* London, California, New Deli, Sage

Carrigan, K (2011) in Milligan, L (2011) *CK's One*, Vogue UK [online] accessed at URL: http://www.vogue.co.uk/news/2011/02/22/calvin-klein-new-ckone-campaign-launch last accessed: 17-8-2011

Carroll, J (2009) *Sexuality Now: Embracing Diversity* Belmont USA, Cengage Learning

Choi, J and Murphy, J (1997) *Postmodernism, unraveling racism, and democratic institutions,* Westport, Praeger Publishers

Clarke (1976) in Hall, S and Jefferson, T (2006) *Resistance through Rituals: youth subcultures in post-war Britain*, New York, Routledge

Clarke, V *et al.* (2010) *Lesbain, Gay, Trans and Queer Psychology: An Introduction*, New York, Cambridge University Press

Cohen, S (1980) *Symbols of Trouble* in Gelder, K (2005) *The Subcultures Reader*, New York, Routledge

Cowell, S (2009) cited in McCormac, P (2009) *Botox for men is on the rise* in The Sunday Times [online] accessed at URL: http://www.timesonline.co.uk/tol/life_and_style/men/article5881581.ece . Last accessed 29-8-2011.

Craddick-Adams, P (2005) *Women at War: 'She-Soldiers' Through the Ages* in BBC History [online] accessed at URL: http://www.bbc.co.uk/history/trail/wars_conflict/home_front/women_at _war_07.shtml last accessed: 15-8-2011

Crane, D (2000) *Fashion and its Social agendas: Class, Gender, and Identity in clothing,* Chicago, University of Chicago Press

Ekins, R (1996) *Blending Genders: Social aspects of cross-dressing and sex-changing,* London, Routledge

Ekins, R and king, D (2006) *The Transgender Phenomenon,* London, California, New Deli, Sage

Elle (2011) *The Runway Edit,* Autumn/Winter edition. London: ELLE.

Gagarina, A (2011) *Transvestism Treatment.* Health AM [online] accessed at URL: http://www.health.am/sex/more/transvestism_ treatment/ last accessed: 22-8-2011

Garber, M (1991) *The Chic of Araby: Transvestism and the Erotics of Cultural Exchange*," *Bodyguards*, eds. Julia Epstein and Kristina Straub New York: Routledge

Garber, M (1992) *Vested Interests: Cross-Dressing and Cultural Anxiety.* New York, Routledge

Halberstam, J (1998) *Drag kings: Masculinity and Performance* K in Gelder, (2005) *The Subcultures Reader*, New York, Routledge

Halberstam, J (2005) *In a queer time and place: transgender bodies, subcultural lives*. New York. New York University Press.

Hebdige, D (1979) *Subculture: The meaning of style*,USA, Methuen & Co.

Hollander, A (1994) *Sex and Suits*. New York, Random House.

http://www.youtube.com/watch?v=iDzzQduDhZg

Kates, G (2001) *Monsieur d'Eon is a woman: A tale of political intrigue and sexual mascarade* Baltimore, Maryland, The John Hopkins University Press

Kuper, A. and Kuper, J (1985) *The Social Science Encyclopaedia,* London and New York, Routledge

Kuzniar, A (1996) *Outing Goethe and his age*, California, Stanford University Press

Lady Gaga (2010) in Furniss, J (2010) 'Too Cool to Care.' *Vogue Hommes, Japan,* September 2010

Loyo, H (1996) *Dietrich's Androgyny and Gendered Spectatorship* in Cornut-Gentille D' Arcy, C and Angel Garcia Landa, J (1996) *Gender, I-deology: essays on theory, fiction and film,* Volume 16 of Postmodern Studies, Radopi

Luscombe, R (2004) *US girls embrace gay passion fashion*, The Guardian [online] accessed at URL: http://www.guardian.co.uk/world/2004/jan/04/usa.gayrights, last accessed: 21-8-2011

MAC (2011) *Viva Glam Campaign History* [online] accessed at URL: http://www.macaidsfund.org/#/glam/campaignhistory last accessed: 21-8-2011

McCormac, P (2009) in Spicer, K and McCormac, P (2009) *Suits you, madam*, Times [online] accessed at URL:http://women.timesonline. co. uk/tol/life_and_style/women/fashion/article5419661.ecelast   accessed: 21-8-2011

Miller, M (1999) *Reexamining Transvestism in Archaic and Classical Athens: The Zewadski Stamnos American Journal of Archaeology*

Milsom, I (2006) *Contraception and Family Planning* Britain, Elsevier

Neisel, D and Herzog, N (2007) *Dr James Barry* in Medical Discovery News [online] accessed at URL: http://www.medicaldiscoverynews.com/ shows/jamesBerry.html last accessed: 15-8-2011

Orenstein, p (2011) *The ghettoisation of pink: how it has cornered the little-girl market* in The Guardian [online] last accessed:22-7-2011 at URL: http://www.guardian.co.uk/society/2011/jun/19/peggy-orenstein-pink-conspiracy-cinderella?INTCMP=SRCH

Ott, B and Mack, R (2009) *Critical Media Studies: An Introduction*, Oxford, Wiley

Paoletti, J (2011) in Orenstein, P (2011) *The ghettoisation of pink: how it has cornered the little-girl market* in The Guardian [online] accessed at URL: http://www.guardian.co.uk/society/2011/jun/19/peggy-orenstein-pink-conspiracy-cinderella. last accessed: 15-8-2011

Perkins, R (1982) *The Drag Queen Scene, Transsexuals in kings Cross* in Ekins, R and king, D (eds) *Blending Genders: Social aspects of cross-dressing and sex-changing.* New York, Routledge

Perrone, D (2007) *Clubbing, Culture, Consumption, Capital and Control: Drug Use Among the New York City Club Kids.* PHD. School of Criminal Justice. The State University of New Jersey

Plummer, K (1996) in Ekins, R and King, D (1996) *Blending Genders: Social aspects of cross-dressing and sex changing.* New York, Routledge.

Quinn, M (2010) in Hattenstone, S (2010) *Marc Quinn: Just don't call it a freak show*, The Guardian [online] accessed at URL:http://www.guardian.co.uk/artanddesign/2010/may/01/marcquinn-interview, last accessed: 21-8-2011

Reingold, H (1994) *Introduction to the Virtual Community* in Gelder, K (2005) *The Subcultures Reader*, New York, Routledge

Sanchez, C (2011) *When sex doesn't* matter, White Ibiza Blog, accessed at URL: http://blog.white-ibiza.com/ibiza-style-boutique-blogger-catherine-sanchez/, last accessed: 21-8-2011

Showalter, E (1992) *Sexual Anarchy, Gender and Culture at the Fin de Siecle,* London, Virago

Singer, T Benjamin (2006) *From the Medical Gaze to Sublime Mutations: The Ethics of (Re)Viewing Non-normative Body Images.* In The Transgender Studies Reader, ed. Susan Stryker and Stephen Whittle. New York: Routledge

Smith, W (2003) *Gay in the 1960s – the time was ripe for revolution*, The Villager [online] accessed at URL: http://www.thevillager.com/villager_8/gayinthe60.html, last accessed 21-8-2011

Steele, V (2010) *The Berg Companion to Fashion.* New York. Berg

Sullivan, J (1997) *2 Men Plead Guilty in Killing of Club Denzien*, NY Times [online] accessed at URL: http://www.nytimes.com/1997/09/11/nyregion/2-men-plead-guilty-in-killing-of-club-denizen.html, last accessed: 21-8-2011

Suthrell, C (2004) *Unzipping Gender*, Oxford, Berg

Torr, D (2002) in Gabriel, B (2002) *Venus Boyz* (press release) [online] accessed at URL: www.venusboyz.com/PDF/presse.pdf. Last accessed: 22-8-2011

Torr, D (2011) *Artist Bio*, Diane Torr [online] accessed at URL: http://www.dianetorr.com/. Last accessed: 22-8-2011

Vol. 103, No. 2 (Apr., 1999), pp. 223-253, Archaeological Institute of America

White, E (1980) *The Political Vocabulary of Homosexuality* in Burke, L and Crowlet, T (2000) *The Routledge Language and Cultural Theory Reader*, London and New York, Routledge

Whitworth, M (2010) *Fashion Blurs Gender Boundaries*, Telegraph [online] accessed at URL: http://fashion.telegraph.co.uk/ news-features/TMG8214923/Fashion-blurs-gender-boundaries.html last accessed 21-8-2011

Woods, H (2010) *Amazons of the ancient world: Women in Greek and Roman societies as seen in the Amazon myth* Theses [online] accessed at URL:http://proquest.umi.com/pqdlink?did=2048105521&Fmt=7&client I d=79356&RQT=309&VName=PQD, last accessed 23-7-2011